WALKING
POINT

R. J. Nevens Jr.

ISBN: 0692507027
ISBN 13: 9780692507025
Library of Congress Control Number: 2015913714
R.J. Nevens, Jr., Kingwood, TX

Photo Credits:
Michelle Steigmeyer
Marine Corps History Division
National Archives
Cover Design by Kevin Coleman

Additional thanks to:
God
Our soldiers, both two- and four-legged
Chelsea Nevens
Larry Chilcoat
Susan Bahary
Kevin B. Coleman
Jeff Helsdon
Olivia Antonello
Mom & Dad
Kristi Kollatschny
Angie Carrizales
William Putney
Betsy Putney

CONTENTS

A marine is always faithful. So is man's best friend.

FOREWORD

This book will bring tears to your eyes as it draws you into the life of our country during World War II. It's an inspiring book based on the author's multi-award-winning screenplay of the same name. It tells two stories: one of a family who gives up their beloved dog for the war effort and another about a young marine who serves alongside this war dog. Both stories take the reader through love, loss, romance, and military history. The book leaves the reader with the feeling that the Greatest Generation earned their name through their bravery and determination to do the right thing at war and at home for the love of their country and freedom.

An entire nation was affected by and contributed to the war effort. Men, women, and children sacrificed their nearest and dearest, including their beloved pet dogs. The author paints a compelling picture of this era and one of the toughest battles of World War II in the Pacific as it weaves throughout the relationships forged among men and between marines and their canine equivalents. It also brings you back to the basics: a simpler, more innocent time and lifestyle in our country's history.

As a sculptor of numerous monuments to the human-animal bond, I feel that the author well understands the special connection that exists between our working dogs and their handlers—and the invaluable, unselfish work they both do. In creating the US War Dog monument, "Always Faithful," I had the honor to know and learn from Captain William W. Putney, veterinarian and head of the 3rd War Dog Platoon on Guam. The monument was dedicated on July 21, 1994, and still resides there today, forever memorializing the brave and heroic efforts of the first US military working dogs and their handlers. Several castings of the monument are located around the country at various universities and museums.

While this book includes many historical accounts of the pain and atrocities that occurred in the Pacific, it is softened by the very touching stories of the undying bond between man and dog. *Walking Point* demonstrates the many ways in which our noble war dogs withstood the rigors of war alongside their heroic handlers, saving the lives of countless US military personnel and civilians. They stood faithfully and fearlessly at the sides of their human counterparts to achieve what could not be achieved without them.

In this book, the characters come to life with seamless dialogue that is often lively and humorous, despite the backdrop of war. This timeless and sensitive account has something for everyone, be it the suffering of war, military history few still know about, romance, or the power of love. It is an important and hopeful account of the human condition and our everlasting connection to our four-footed faithful companions. It is truly a story of love, loss, and victory. This book is summed up in two very simple sentences: A marine is always faithful. So is man's best friend.

Susan Bahary
Bahary Studios, Inc.
www.baharystudios.com
California

1

LITTLE ROCK

John Markle ran his fingers over the top of the granite stone, paying careful attention to the horse's mane. The stone, warmed from the sun, felt soothing against his young skin, reminding him of his mother's touch. He knelt down next to the ornate statue and clipped the overgrown weeds and grass away. Meticulously, he trimmed back the uninvited intruders. He wouldn't allow them to conceal any amount of his mother's memory.

It had been a week or so since he'd visited her final resting place. His father worked long hours to afford it. It was still untouched by the weather and had retained its magnificence over the years. A large piece of granite with a carved stallion's head sparkled in the light of the setting sun. The horse's mane was carved to mimic it flowing in the wind of a full-stride gallop. The only shade was cast by a stoic, old oak tree. It had seen him visit the grave on many occasions, watching John transform from a young boy into a determined and ambitious young man.

He read her tombstone out loud. "Betty Ann Markle. Born June 15, 1906. Died February 17, 1937. Loving mother, loving wife, loved her family, loved her life."

The dwindling sunlight cut his visit short. He had visited his mother's grave at least once a week since she'd passed. Over time, his tears had turned to smiles. He had grown comfortable with her absence. He had accepted the cards that life had dealt her. He didn't blame God, himself, his father—or anyone, for that matter. His honor and love for his mother were tucked away in his heart, and they made him smile inside. He always wanted to make her proud.

He leaned down, kissed the granite stallion, and said, "Love you, Momma. One day. One day." He grabbed the lead to his horse and took mount.

"John! Come on home! Dinner's ready!" Roy Markle, his father, yelled from across the daisy-lidded field. Orange rust fell from the triangle as he flailed it hard enough to echo through the hills.

John spurred his horse and, with a cloud of dust, hustled home to see what his father had cooked up. Their family farm was first worked by John's grandfather, who, with the help of his wife and two other sons, worked the hundred and ten acres year round. The land was plush, properly farmed, and used to raise cattle. It also provided a great place for John and his high school friends to participate in their homemade war games. They would dress in their fathers' gear and play a more intense version of hide-and-seek, complete with booby traps and fireworks. The farm was affected when John's grandfather passed away, along with both of John's uncles. Roy was the only one to survive the accident. Their family was one of the few that owned a tractor; actually, it was shared with two other local families to help with the cost of owning such a large, expensive machine. Most farming at that time, the late 1920s, was done with mules and horses. The increased production came at the ultimate cost when John's grandfather suffered a heart attack while driving the tractor and subsequently ran it into the threshing machine. His two uncles were working on the loud machine and couldn't hear John yell to them as he watched the tractor plow into them, crushing their bodies.

Then, just a few years later, the Great Depression hit, and farming, already tough due to major drought conditions, was sent into a downward spiral. They had to sell off thirty acres of land, but they still maintained the majority of the good farming land.

The dinner bell was clanking in the background as John looked back at the old oak—now the guardian of this sacred spot. The triangle's effort to push its sound waves off the surrounding canyon walls was effective. The echoes effortlessly rang throughout the hills. The clanking, coupled with the full-stride rhythmic pounding of the horse's hooves, reminded him of times his mother would ring the bell and call him home for supper. His father was an excellent cook but couldn't hold a candle to his mother's way of making fricasseed chicken with brown rice or Kentucky succotash. Her homemade rice pudding was everyone's favorite. Neighbors who lived acres away would come over to indulge when word got out that she was making it. Sometimes they would make excuses just to show up and ask if they could borrow a cup of milk or a little bit of cream. Betty would just smile, knowing they were all excuses to come over to get a bowl of the pudding, the most famous pudding in Pulaski County.

Never mind that they all lived on working farms with cows, enough cows to conjure up plenty of their own cream and milk. She took it as a compliment, and the visits gave Roy the opportunity to solicit help with chores around the aging farm. A bowl of her rice pudding was an extremely fair trade to help mend a fence or patch a hole in the barn.

"Hey, Son," said Roy as he stared at him, "how's your mother?"

"She's fine. Resting easy."

"You get it all cleaned up?"

"Yes, sir. What's the chow tonight, Pops?" he asked, pointing to the stove.

Since the war had started, food was being rationed, and the Great Depression hit the states hard. All the chicken farmers, at the direction of the government, had diverted their supplies to the war effort. Chicken was hard to come by, and most of their own met their ends at the mouths of coyotes. The ones left were strictly for their eggs and lived their lives in the confines of a fence encompassing a small, smelly, wooden coop.

"Guess." Roy smiled and raised one eyebrow comically.

"It's not that hard. I'll say skillet steak."

"Skillet steak? We just had that last night."

"And the night before. And the night before that." John placed his hand on his dad's shoulder. "It's all right, Pops. I'm just happy to be eating."

Roy interrupted and exclaimed in a proud tone, "Fricasseed chicken!"

John's face lit up. His father never attempted to make that dish before. "It smells great. So one of the chickens is gone?"

"Dead as a doornail and smelling better than a bottle of Coty L'Origan." He was proud of what he'd accomplished. "I used two of her eggs as well. That chicken is feeding us good tonight. A little onion, carrot, celery, and some thyme and parsley. I even borrowed some lemon juice from Wallace down the way." He stirred the pot, allowing the aroma to fill the tiny kitchen.

"Well, shoot. Let's get it in our stomachs."

"Take a seat, Son. Milk?

"Yes, sir."

Roy brought the food over and set it down on the table. He took his seat across from John. They both stared at each other for a few seconds, relishing the special moment they were sharing. It wasn't very often they both were quiet, but this moment in time, this moment of recollection, was theirs.

John broke the comfortable silence. "Let's say a prayer for Mom." He reached over and grabbed his dad's hand. Their callused hands cradled each other.

They were both God-fearing men, but daily prayer wasn't something that typically occurred in their household. They rarely went to church—maybe once every couple of months—and they'd make a day of it, stopping at the grocery and feed store, and occasionally seeing a few friends in town. Roy agreed without hesitation.

"Dear God," John Began. "I don't pray near enough, so please forgive me for that. Forgive *us* for that. We love you. You are the reason for our being. We question things that happen in our lives, but in the end the plan is all yours. We are just a part of it. Lord, tell Mom hi for us. I know she is with you. Please forgive us for our transgressions and trespasses. Bless this food for the nourishment of our bodies. In Jesus's name we pray. Amen."

Roy reached over to pat John on the shoulder. He quietly whispered, "Amen."

His father wept silently inside, not only for the past loss of his wife, the only woman he'd ever loved, but

from what he knew John was about to tell him. He knew
the time was here, the time when his son, mature as he
already was, would become a man and go from shooting deer and coyotes to dodging the enemy's grenades
and bullets. Roy knew the horrors that war placed on a
young man. He was reluctantly optimistic, hoping for
a safe return. He could see the nervousness in John's
eyes. Or was it excitement? Perhaps a combination of
both. John was an adventurous young man, always the
first to step up and take the dare. His six-foot frame,
held up by his broad shoulders and square hips, was
combat-ready. John was in notable shape and favored a
good challenge. His physical prowess, coupled with his
intelligence, would serve him well in the US Marines.
His square jaw, tense from the words about to leave his
mouth, began to open. He was interrupted.

"John, I love you, Son. I know what you're about to
say."

"Dad, let me—"

"Hold on now. Let me say my piece first."

John prepared for his father's words. He sat back in
the old, creaky, wooden chair, ears open to his hero's
advice.

"I believe in you. I know what you're about to tell
me. I found this in your room." He threw an enlistment form on the table.

"Dad—"

"I'm proud of you, Son. It takes guts to do what
you're doing. To fight for what's right. To give without

expecting anything in return. I knew you were cut out for this years ago. Your mother was still alive, you remember? She wasn't too fond of us going shooting. You remember that?"

"Yes, sir," John said with his crooked grin. "It was the first time I shot a gun."

"It was. You knocked that can right off that damned fence, and that gun knocked you on your tail!" He laughed out loud, reminiscing about that youthful experience shared with his only son.

"You remember Mom's face when she saw my black eye?"

"Do I ever."

"We tried to hide that shiner for days."

"She knew the day it happened," he said as he glanced over at her photo. "She didn't say anything. She knew you were proud of that black eye."

Perhaps his father was too. It was a badge of honor, the mark of some ritual transforming him from a boy to a man. He wore that black eye like a cowboy wore his cowboy hat: boastfully, full of hauteur, begging the world to look at him and feel his cavalier virility, as much as an eleven-year-old could at least. He had grown up since those days. John Markle was born to be a soldier—and a comely one at that.

"Tell me, John," he asked, "what makes you want to join the marines?" He already knew the answer. He had seen all the qualities John displayed throughout his youth. Naturally, he wanted to hear it from his son, to know that he knew it was a life-changing decision, one that had severe consequences and could very well take his life. The United States had adopted the conscription. John was not one to let someone else determine his tomorrow, much less his future years. College wasn't in his future. Financially, they couldn't afford it, and socially, it just wasn't for John.

"Dad, I can wait for them to call me up, or I can go ahead and get in there and try to make a change, a difference," he said valiantly. "I'm not trying to be a hero. I'm just trying to do what I think will make Mom proud—what will make you proud."

"Son, I couldn't be more proud of you than I am right now. I know your mother is proud of you. She always was." Roy poked the fireplace, and he stared into the fervent flames. They fluttered around the glowing embers, much the way his thoughts were fluttering through his mind. He had concerns, but an unyielding man doesn't let that show. He had to place those doubts down deep and concede them to his manhood. "I believe that you can make a difference—that you can help people. You're a leader, Son. You always have been. I'd be proud to tell everyone my son is a marine, fighting for those who cannot fight for themselves."

"I'm proud to call you my father," John stated with utmost confidence. "I won't let you down. I know it's hard, but I feel it in my gut—like it's calling me, like something is pulling at my heartstrings. I may die out there. I know that's an option. I'm willing to accept that. God knows my fate. He controls my destiny, but I control my rifle."

They continued their conversation throughout the night, talking about everything, laughing about some things, and grieving over others. They bonded that night like they never had. It was a love John had not experienced from his father.

No matter what he said, he knew his father stood beside him, cared for him, and loved him. It was a true display of unconditional love. An unforgettable love. John's father had lived a life of loss. He'd lost friends in World War I, lost his own father, his two brothers, and his wife. Life was not easy for him, and it took strength to survive. It took faith to maintain his sanity, and it took love to conquer all obstacles that had been placed in front of him. Talking to his father all night helped John rid himself of the guilt he felt for leaving his dad—or most of it, at least.

2

A089

It was good to be eight years old and not have a care in the world, at least not one that would move beyond losing your Slinky or getting your Silly Putty stuck in your hair. This newfound product was remarkable. It could stretch forever, bounce as high as the sky, and remarkably transpose newspaper print onto itself. These miraculous feats amazed Tommy Johnson. Its plastic, egg-shaped shell kept it safe and allowed him to tote it around everywhere.

The war effort made it hard to find good toys. Many factories stopped producing consumer products and focused on fabricating weapons and military-based products. That's why Tommy loved his Silly Putty. It was actually a product of that effort, an ineffectual one to produce a synthetic plastic, and that led to a wondrous product beloved by every child. Children across the United States used it to lift comics right from the comic pages. It was magic. And as thousands of parents across the country realized, it took magic to get it out of their kids' hair.

But Silly Putty was second on his list of favorites. The blue-eyed, blond-haired Tommy loved the little army men. The pint-sized, two-inch-tall Benton military figures were just the right size and would often displace the Silly Putty in his pocket. Who needed Silly Putty when you had army men? There was a war to be won. It started in the Johnson's backyard. Tommy had command of his own army, his own troops. They were at his beck and command. None of them dared disobey the orders of Sergeant Tommy, or there would be hell to pay. You could be buried alive or drowned in the creek, crushed by a rock, or tied to a tree and left to the carnivorous insects. Your lack of respect for the adolescent orders of Sergeant Johnson could also land you in the worst scenario of all: in the crushing jaws of the mystical creature that roamed the battlefields outside the protective walls of Fort Johnson. Any little green army man who had witnessed this slobbering, saber-toothed, four-legged monstrosity met his Maker within seconds.

"You! Private Bazooka!" squawked the eight-year-old sergeant, his imagination running wild. He grabbed the little Benton figure—who was aptly named because he carried a bazooka hoisted on his shoulder. "What do you think you're doin'? I thought

I told you to clean the latrines!" Tommy yelled in his best military voice.

He responded to himself as the bazooka soldier, "Yes sir, but I didn't think they was dirty." His voice carried a cowardly overtone. He now had his army man in one hand and the bazooka soldier in the other—face to face, mano a mano.

"Soldier, that was an order! I guess you want to end up like Private Lookout, huh?" Again, Private Lookout was aptly named for his statuesque kneeling position and binoculars. While the names weren't that creative, they served their purpose for identification.

"Sir, anything but that! I didn't mean any—" Bazooka tried to finish but was cut off.

"This is the last time. You're going to meet your Maker today!" Tommy said as he shook his replica self authoritatively.

"No! No!" Tommy voiced as Bazooka.

There are no rules in child warfare. Tommy didn't need to have German soldiers or Japanese troops. His irrational childish wrath was unforgiving—humorous, but unforgiving. In fact, Private Lookout was fed to the creature outside the walls for simply not acknowledging Sergeant Johnson just the week before. The only figurine that constantly escaped the young boy's authority was Sergeant Salute. He was always kissing ass, and he got preferred treatment from Tommy.

"Come with me," Tommy said. "You will meet the creature I call Duke."

"No! No!" cried Tommy in his best frightened-Bazooka voice.

Tommy stood up—he too was dressed in army gear—and walked over to the large oak tree, his eyes scanning the horizon of the large backyard.

"Duke!" Tommy yelled, but there was no response. He waited for a few seconds, and then called again.

"Help!" he exclaimed as Bazooka.

"Nothing can help you!" Tommy said in a sinister tone. "Duke!"

He looked around again—but nothing. Certainly the creature was around, possibly hiding in the brush, waiting, and stalking his next victim. Maybe an ambush was imminent? Maybe today the creature had decided to exert complete control over the backyard—over Fort Johnson, and its master, Sergeant Tommy Johnson? He could feel eyes upon him. Just then he was knocked to the ground. A rush of controlled energy and furry mass toppled him to the ground.

"Duke!" Tommy shouted. "Come here. Good boy, Duke. Good boy." He completely forgot about serving Private Bazooka to the wretched creature. He rolled around on the ground with Duke, playfully rubbing his pointed ears.

"How do you always sneak up on me, boy?" he said. "You're so good."

Duke was a beautiful one-and-a-half-year-old Doberman pinscher. He was their cherished family pet. Duke was the poster child for the breed: large paws, extremely attentive, smart, and loyal. And his markings made him all but invisible at night, especially when the moon's illuminating beams failed to reach the ground, casting the shadows of the trees hindering their advancement.

"Come here, boy." Tommy placed his father's old marine Brodie helmet back on his head and straightened it up. He and Duke sat next to each other. Duke scooted closer to his human counterpart, seeking comfort, praise, and admiration. They were facing back at the little army men's Fort Johnson, the tiny soldiers scattered all about in disarray, some lying on the ground and others manning the small cardboard walls of the five-inch-high fort. All types of soldiers were standing ready as well, including Private Grenade Thrower, Private Bugle, Private Gas Mask, Private Infantry, and Private Rifleman. Tommy's focus went to the little dog figurine. It was out of place—obviously not a Benton. In fact, he had just added it to the fort a few days ago. He thought the soldiers needed a dog to keep them company while they fought. It was a little ceramic German shepherd, disproportionate to the Benton soldiers, so much that it was just as tall as the soldier figurines, much like a horse.

"Duke, you'd make a good soldier," Tommy said sincerely to his best friend. "I love you, boy."

He got up and placed his Sergeant Tommy Johnson army figurine next to the dirty, chipped shepherd. The level ground wouldn't allow for him to stay up, so he symbolically leaned them against each other. His parents watched from the kitchen window as their son continued to play with Duke. Ty, a former marine himself, had served his country proudly and still maintained the "high and tight" haircut. He experienced the hardships of the early 1900s and wanted better for his family. Life was dealing his family a tough hand—one that wouldn't allow him to trade in three cards and get three new ones. He had a full house, but that was in life. His poker hand now was one to fold, though Ty was not a quitter—not by any stretch of the imagination. He had worked hard to get to where he was. He would overcome this obstacle.

He had the support of his beautiful wife, Sherry. She was a native of Illinois. She displayed the character of Rosie the Riveter, but she had the elegance of Mae West. Her light blond hair and fair skin made her simply radiant in the afternoon sun. The light reflected gently from her shiny locks. She stood out in any room.

"Look at him out there," he said. "How are we supposed to tell him?"

He was not looking forward to breaking the news to Tommy. He had lost his job several months before—nothing of his own doing, but a victim of hard times. Like so many others, he was laid off.

"Honey, we can handle this," Sherry stated with a compassionate voice. "We're tough."

They continued to watch Tommy and Duke through the large picture window. Tommy loved that dog. Ty tossed a newspaper down on the pine-topped coffee table. A "Dogs for Defense" advertisement was face up:

Dogs for Defense. Does Your Dog Want To Be a Hero?

With a deep breath Ty said, "I'll call him in."

Sherry vacated the room, anticipating what was about to happen. She was tough. They both were. But there's nothing easy about telling a young boy his best friend was about to leave to go to war.

"Tommy! Come on in, Son. It's time to eat," Ty yelled from the back door.

Tommy and Duke came running, and Tommy said, while out of breath, "Duke found me every time today, Dad."

"Come on in here," Ty said as he patted his boy on the helmet.

Duke slipped by them, losing traction on the hard-wood floor but managing to get to his food bowl. "He's pretty good at hide and seek, huh?"

"Yes, sir," Tommy replied as he straightened the doughboy helmet on his head. He loved to wear it, but it mainly impeded his vision and was the root cause for many of his bumps, bruises, and scrapes.

"He's really good at playing army too?"

"He's an eager beaver, Dad. The cat's meow."
Tommy loved to use words and phrases he heard on
the radio. The family would lie around and listen to
Abbott and Costello on Wednesday nights. Tommy
would try to mimic their roundabout comedy style. But
what he really looked forward to were the times his father would let him listen to *The Whistler*. It was between
father and son, and not to be shared with his mom.
The crime melodrama, full of tales of mystery and
terror, was not for the faint of heart, and it typically
caused a sleepless night for the young patriot. Tommy,
being the smart and antagonizing child he was, would
occasionally end one of his stories, typically involving
Duke and their backyard adventures, by saying in a sinister voice, "a strange ending to tonight's story."

That was the sign-off of *The Whistler*, and it always
followed a twisted tale of furor and mayhem. He would
watch his mother as he said it, just to see if he could
get a reaction. He would then look over at his father
with a covert smile, acknowledging their weekly secret
liturgy. To him, just as to any young boy, it was exciting
to keep a secret. It made it even better when Ty would
tell him, "Don't you dare tell your mother about this,"
reinforcing the confidentiality and severity of their
clandestine actions.

"Son, come over here and take a seat," Ty requested. He knew this was a tough conversation to have.

"Okay, Dad," Tommy replied. "Duke! Come on, boy."

They both crashed into the couch, with Duke piling up on top of Tommy. Duke was a "leaner" too. He leaned on his companion, resting peacefully at his side, waiting for Tommy to give praise in the form of an ear rub. It came quickly just as Ty and Sherry joined them. Ty took his seat next to them. He wrapped his arm around Tommy, reaching far enough to rub Duke's ear as well.

"Son, life is full of really hard decisions," Ty started.

Sherry, already feeling overwhelmed with emotion, quickly stood up and walked to the other room, hiding her tears from them.

"What's wrong with Mom?" Tommy inquired, following her with his worried eyes.

"She's sad. I'm sad too," Ty replied. "Son, life is full of adventures—good and bad—and sometimes with those adventures come decisions that are both good and bad. Sometimes those decisions lead people to set things free—things they love dearly, things they don't want to let go. And when you have to make one of those tough decisions, you hope and pray, Son, that those things come back to you."

Tommy, understanding the concept but not the situation, asked, "Are you and mom going to be like Sammy's parents?" There aren't too many worries for an eight-year-old, but the look on Tommy's face was indicative of someone distressed and uneasy.

"Oh no, no, Tommy. Nothing like that."

Sammy lived down the road and was Tommy's friend. Sammy's parents had divorced just months before, and Sammy was forced to move with his mother two towns over. They hadn't seen each other since.

"Then what's wrong with Mom? Why is she crying?"

He held Tommy tighter and said, "We had to make one of those tough decisions, a really tough decision. We're moving, Son."

"Where to?"

"Lassister Hills. About forty-five miles north."

"Is there woods for Duke and me to play?"

Sherry entered the room and placed a box of tissues on the table, her nose red from sobbing.

"We love you, Son. Dukes loves you, but we can't take him with us. We tried to find a place for him, but nothing worked out. Lasister Hills are apartments, and they don't allow animals."

Sherry moved over next to Tommy and Duke and hugged them. They all sat on the couch, huddled up— their own unit, and their own family company.

"So where is Duke going?" Tommy asked, worried about his best friend.

"We tried to find a place, Tommy. We tried hard," Sherry said.

"We did have one option that we thought you would like."

"I don't like any of it," Tommy replied honestly.

Ty jumped in. "Well, Son, you know that Duke loves to play hide-and-seek and army, right?"

"Yep, and he's good at hunting those squirrels, too." The words rolled proudly from his tongue.

"And he's smart as the dickens, right?"

"Yep."

"And the United States is fighting a war right now and needs everyone to help protect us?" Ty said, trying to reinforce the decision.

"From the Japs?"

"Yes, Son. From the Japs."

"Well, Duke doesn't understand Japanese, so he can't go there," Tommy bluntly stated.

His words inserted a little bit of laughter into the situation. The seriousness of his eight-year-old tone was evident.

"Son, Duke is going to be a volunteer military dog. He's going to help keep us safe. And when he's done, he can come back to us. A soldier dog. A hero. Our Duke, a hero-soldier dog. There is no way you could ever hide from him again."

"A hero like you, Dad?" Tommy rubbed his old helmet.

"Yes, Son. A hero like your old man."

3

GOOD-BYE

"So what d'ya think, Duke?" asked Tommy. He gazed around his bedroom, pondering the situation at hand, contemplating all the scenarios that could play out, a tactical movement he had witnessed his dad play out many times. One such time was their teamwork as tree trimmers. The massive oak in their backyard had a dead limb that needed to come down due to a storm a few months earlier that had caused damage in town and toppled trees. This oak, an exceptionally large white oak, standing seventy feet tall and encompassing a diameter of fifty feet from limb to limb, cast a welcome amount of shade in the hot summer sun.

Their task was to trim the dead branch hanging twenty feet above the ground. Mother Nature couldn't hurt this tree; she couldn't even knock the dead branch down. Although the tree swayed wildly in the grasp of the storm, the gusting straight-line winds failed in their crusade to handicap this permanent earthly fixture.

Tommy petted Duke. He clutched his little Benton army figure in his other hand as he reflected on that day. He recalled the conversation he'd had with his dad.

"Tommy, this is a dangerous job. Are you up to the task?" Ty, playing the part of a construction foreman, asked.

"Of course. Let's get to choppin' and sawin', Pop!"

"Well, just hold on there. We've got to plan this out—you know, take a second to think it through. For instance, we could just jump right in, both of us climb up that tree and start sawin'. But then there's no one to keep watch, to make sure the limb doesn't fall and hurt anyone." Ty kept on rationalizing the situation and the particular scenarios. "So that doesn't work. We could send you up there to cut by yourself. But you're not gonna last too long. You're a good climber, just a bit too fragile. See, I'm not a great climber, but I can saw right through that puny limb. You got to be able to recognize all the possible scenarios, not just taking this limb down. Most decisions in life require some sort of rational thought. Place importance on what the overall goal is, and factor in safety, logic, and making the work as effective and easy as possible. You accept that rationale, however you get there in your mind, then act on it. Never second-guess it, Son.

Indecision at the wrong time will never help you. It tricks your mind."

Tommy, still sitting quietly, leaned in toward his dad. He put his hand on his father's shoulder and said, "Let's not sit here with your gobbledygook. Let's cut down a tree!" Tommy joked as he mimicked an arborist apprentice, overzealous in his expectations.

"I'm glad you got your boots on, Son. You're a chip off the old block."

Tommy's memory was interrupted by a soft knock at his door. Duke, accustomed to this distraction, barely lifted an eyebrow. He did manage to exert some energy to turn his cropped ear in the direction of the quiet knock, if only for a second. In Duke's eyes, the soft noise didn't even call for a lifting of his head. His head just lay on the pillow, unaware his destiny had been changed just hours ago. Home was about to change.

"Tommy?" The compassion in Sherry's voice filled the room. "Hi. Can I come in?"

She walked over and took a seat on the edge of the bed. She picked up the "Dogs for Defense" advertisement. The edges were curled on both ends, mainly from Tommy's hands cupping the paper as he read it, which probably had happened hundreds of times in the past few hours. She was taken aback to see that Tommy wasn't crying.

He began to recite the advertisement verbatim, front and back. Sherry looked at him. It took her a few seconds, but then she realized it. She had always thought so, but at this moment, this small grain of sand in the hourglass of time revealed something to her. Tommy was going to grow up to do wondrous things. She let her shoulders relax from the tension they had been holding for some time. She drew him near and hugged him, glad the secret about Duke's enlistment was finally out in the open.

"Oh, Tommy, you are such a brave young man. Duke will be okay." She reinforced what Tommy had already made fact in his mind. They lay there together until the early morning, when the sound of grinding gears woke them up.

Ty, who had joined the sleep-over sometime in the night, opened his tired eyes first. Duke stood in the window, looking down from the two-story view. He turned to look at Ty for a second and then back to the window. The sound of a slamming car door brought Ty out of bed and woke the others from their slumber.

Typically, Duke would be downstairs barking but today was different. Was Duke aware of something? Had his senses told him something was a brew? He was certainly calmer than normal, almost displaying a degree of certainty, as if he were ready for this task.

"Who is it?" Sherry asked as she rubbed her eyes. She asked the question, knowing what the answer was going to be. She was being routine, going through the motions, and starting that day, hoping for a different sequence of events.

Ty turned to her and said, "It's them."

Duke turned from the window and trotted through the bedroom door and down the wooden stairs. He stopped and waited for them at the bottom, the clacking of his nails against the floors echoed one last time throughout their home. Ty, Sherry, and Tommy all looked at one another and began their journey downstairs. Tommy stopped and grabbed a picture frame from the small table at the bottom. It was a picture of him and Duke the day they had brought him home. He was just a young pup then, with large paws that were out of proportion to his legs. His ears were still natural, and his head was charmingly larger than his body.

"Well, Duke, today this little puppy becomes a soldier," Tommy said.

Ty asked, "You okay, Tommy?"

"Yes, just sad."

"It's a lot to take in, Son. It's hard to say good-bye to your friend. We can't imagine our life without him, either. But he'll be back. They'll bring him back."

"Dad, I don't want him to go now," Tommy cried out in love for Duke.

Duke had grown up with them, and while most families would rarely allow their dog to loiter indoors, the Johnsons loved to have Duke roaming their hallways. They just felt safer. Duke even gave Ty a sense of ease, allowing for long nights of sleep with the windows open. Certainly, Duke would let them know if someone or something trespassed into their territory. Thankfully, that theory was never tested, perhaps because Ty, as trusting as he was, would only leave the second-story windows ajar. He was going to miss Duke. He always slept better knowing that his family alarm, bodyguard, and protector was there. But he would not be with them tonight. It was hard for him to be the rock right now. But his family needed him to be strong, didn't they?

Sherry knew Ty had a soft streak. She knew it was going to come out. He spent too much time with Duke, and Tommy, to not let this bother him, to ruffle the hardened exterior he displayed daily. That's why Sherry loved him so.

She knew what peeled back his armor. Ever since they decided they had to move, Ty had been more attached to Duke. He even helped defend the imaginary Fort Johnson with Duke and Tommy on a few occasions. He and Sherry tried so hard to find a nice temporary home for Duke. They had no family for hundreds of miles and no takers locally. Their efforts met no success. It was just by fate one day that Ty opened the newspaper right to the advertisement about Dogs for Defense. That was forty-five days ago to the date. They were both relieved that Tommy now knew but so sad that the time was finally here for them to officially part ways. Ty thought on many levels this was the right thing to do. There's a reason that advertisement was in that paper, and while he knew Tommy was patriotic, he did not expect such support from Tommy. He was happy his son was embracing the idea—sadly embracing it, but embracing it nonetheless.

"It's okay, Son. Do you want to spend some time with him? It's all right. We can do what you want if you want some time," Ty said.

Tommy wrapped his arms around Duke and buried his head in his neck, holding him for dear life. He could only accept what was happening, his young mind reeling with emotions. Ty and Sherry comforted him as they all huddled with Duke and let their emotions boil to the surface. This was a moment they would never forget. It was interrupted by the rap at the front door. They wiped their tears and all walked to the front of the house.

Ty grabbed the doorknob and reluctantly pulled it open. There in the doorway stood two US Marines, at attention, with welcoming smiles. They had to smile. A situation this delicate required the utilization of every personable and human trait. Anything that could help ease the pain and the second-guessing that comes with this decision was welcome in their arsenal. They were marines. They could adapt to any situation. Their mission here was to comfort the Johnsons—and bring Duke back with them.

"Good morning, ma'am. Good morning, sir. I'm Sergeant Tibbs. This here is Sergeant Jones." Tibbs extended his right hand to Ty and removed his hat with the other, respecting the proper introduction to a woman.

Ty lifted his hand to his forehead, saluting his fellow marine, and said, "I'm Ty. This my wife, Sherry."

The marines graciously said, "Ma'am," as they tipped their heads.

"This is Tommy, Duke's best friend," Ty stated.

"Oh yes, Tommy. I've heard a lot about you, young man." Sergeant Tibbs extended his hand, but Tommy followed his dad's lead and saluted. The marines saluted back. Tibbs noticed Tommy staring at his gun.

"You like guns?"

Tommy nodded his head.

"Guns help the good guys keep things good. Tommy, I've talked to your mother and father, and we are happy to have Duke. From what I hear, we're lucky to have him. He's going to make a great soldier, and he'll learn a lot through the Dogs for Defense program. I know you love Duke. Are you okay with him becoming a soldier?" Sergeant Tibbs questioned.

Duke began to lick Tommy and paw at him for attention. Tommy asked, "So what will he be doing?"

"Duke will be protecting our country. He'll undergo extensive training, but from what your parents tell me, he's already an expert at sniffing you out."

"He is, and he finds me every time. He finds my dad, too."

"He does," Ty chimed in.

"Well, Tommy, and family, I can promise you we will keep him safe," Sergeant Tibbs said. "And when Duke is done protecting our country, we will bring him back to you, a soldier dog. He's going to be part of the first war-dog platoons."

Tommy, intrigued by the marine's words, let them soak in. He waited for a few dramatic seconds, and then replied, "The president says we need all the help we can muster. I heard him on the radio, and that's what he said."

"So, Tommy, what do you think?" Ty asked.

Tommy looked at Duke, then up at the marines, and said, "I'm okay with him going with you, sir."

"I promise you again, Son, we will take care of Duke," Sergeant Tibbs replied. "I give you my word— the word of a marine and the word of your father. We will keep him safe."

With that, the marine leaned in to grab the leash, but Tommy quickly threw his arm in front and said, "Wait! I want to pray for Duke."

"Of course, Tommy," Sherry said.

They huddled around Duke, even the marines, and Tommy began to pray.

"Dear God. I hope that you can hear me right now. Please keep Duke safe in his real-life game of hide-and-seek. I really want him to come back safe. I want the soldiers to be safe, too. I also pray that you will help Mom and Dad get a new house so that when Duke comes back he has a place to play. Please make sure the house has a lot of woods. Duke likes to play in the woods. In Jesus's name we pray. Amen."

"Amen," the group followed.

The entire group had tears in their eyes. They watched Duke walk away with the marines. Even the toughest people are susceptible to emotion when a family pet is involved. Tibbs walked away with Duke, but he couldn't look back in their direction. He was reminded of the time he was a young boy, and his dog left and never returned. He tried hard to hold it back but one lone tear forced its way to the surface and squeezed itself from his marine-tough tear duct.

Ty ran over to them quickly. He wanted to give them a little history lesson on Duke. Tibbs was taken by surprise when Ty caught him wiping away the tear. He comforted Tibbs by telling him, as an older marine, that he too cried. He had seen men killed in action in front of him, but nothing was more heartrending than the loss of a dog, a best friend. He explained to them that Duke came from a pure bloodline and was born in Indiana to two remarkable Dobermans. They'd brought him home for Tommy for his birthday a year and half ago. He was expensive, but the loss of money meant nothing when Tommy and Duke were introduced. They were instantly best friends. Just as a boy and his dog should be, they were inseparable. Tommy had never been without Duke since. They slept together, played together, and they even ate together sometimes outside.

"Bring Duke back safe."

4

EMILY

Emily Hutchins was a beautiful and highly intelligent young lady who volunteered her time with Dogs for Defense. The program was started by a well-known poodle breeder, and Emily joined Dogs for Defense after a brief stint with the American Kennel Club. She initially helped the program by placing ads in popular magazines, recruiting celebrities to endorse the group, but she fell back to her love of animals and began helping the dogs transition from the program and into the care of the armed forces. Her loyalty and dedication to the animals was obvious from the start. They brought her on staff, and she quickly became the best trainer the program employed.

Duke was transported to the program after the marines picked him up from the Johnsons. From there he had trained at a camp on Cat Island located in Gulfport, Mississippi. The humid semitropical weather there made it ideal for training the dogs and preparing them for the environment and climate of the Pacific. Duke and Emily first met there when he was assigned to her training group.

He was a natural, and perhaps even more so due to his suburban war games with Tommy. He mastered all of the brief training drills administered by the program. While their preparation was good, what lay ahead of them in basic training with the marines would be more strenuous, difficult, and demanding. Many dogs simply weren't meant to be in the program and were sent back to their owners. Too much depended on their specialized skill set. If they couldn't master and perfect them, people, including soldiers, would perish. Once the dogs completed the training in Gulfport, Duke boarded a train and made his way, along with Emily, to Camp Lejeune, North Carolina.

The old steam train blew its whistle one last time as it pulled into Jacksonville, North Carolina, just miles away from Camp Lejeune. The wind was ferocious. The sixty-foot pine trees swayed back and forth with the direction of the vortex, some breaking and losing their tops. The club car was full of crates that were in turn filled with dogs. They were barking, howling, and cowering at the threat the storm posed. Duke, however, sat resilient in the face of danger. His crate, placed by the open door, had a full view of the chaos taking place outside. The occasional tree branch or garbage can would fly by and hit the train car, some even managing to find their way inside, colliding with their crates. The rain was beginning to fall heavily. The sky was spitting large water drops that sounded like metal pellets when they hit the train. Immediately, hail began to fall. Golf-ball-sized chunks of frozen projectiles turned their camp into a war zone, and Mother Nature turned from friend to foe. The large hail was breaking windows and bludgeoning the people who couldn't find shelter fast enough. The wind was so strong it was pushing the rain sideways. In the distance, a loud horn sounded. It was faint and hard to hear over the howling wind and the constant ping of hail ricocheting off the train. It blended in with the panicked screams of the people at the station. It was the dreaded tornado siren.

"Seek shelter now!" yelled one person as he ran past frantically. "There's a tornado heading straight for us!"

Emily came running past, making the decision to hop into the train car with the dogs. She grabbed hold of the doorway and began to pull herself up and in. She was face-to-face with Duke. Still stoic in his expression, he lifted his upper lip to reveal his teeth and let out a little growl.

"Oh, nice to see you again," she said, unshaken by his display of dominance. "Calm down, because I'm coming in!" She yelled over the mayhem.

She grabbed the side and began to hoist herself up. She turned back to look in the direction of the sound of an incoming train. It wasn't a train. The ominous roar hailed from a violent rotating column of air and debris, blackening the sky and throwing everything in its path skyward. The translucent dust surrounding the funnel seemed to multiply its size. Emily's eyes widened as she saw the tornado closing in. Just at that moment a huge pine tree crashed into the side of the train car, throwing her to the ground and knocking her head on the concrete platform. A few crates tumbled from the doorway, including Duke's, shattering violently, and releasing him from the confines of the small cell. A few other dogs shared the same fate. They instinctively made haste in the opposite direction of the twister. Duke, to the contrary, ran over to Emily and began to tug her under the train and into safety. Pulling Emily, who couldn't have weighed more than one hundred fifteen pounds, was a tough task for Duke.

He gripped her belt and dragged her, but the belt broke, leaving them both in the open and susceptible to injury. The twister was closing in. The roar was unbearable. The ground was shaking, and the station lights were flickering. The pulsing lights stopped abruptly just as the tornado siren became inaudible. The siren was hundreds of feet in the air by now. Emily, slowly regaining consciousness, was grabbed and dragged under the train quickly by an unfamiliar hand. Duke instinctively followed. They all cowered under the protection of the thousands of pounds of steel. The young soldier covered Duke and Emily with his body, unselfishly sheltering them from the finger of God. Emily raised her head only to see the bottom of the funnel a few hundred feet away. She began screaming as loudly as she could, not necessarily from fear but from excitement and adrenaline. The soldier palmed the base of her skull.

"Keep your head down!" He screamed over the roar. He started yelling as loud as he could back at the tornado, releasing the built-up adrenaline rush.

The train was shaking violently. The large metal wheels bounced around on the tracks as the straight-line winds pounded the sides of the cars. The dogs that remained in the train car had stopped howling and barking, literally scared silent. The roar was deafening. The air was teeming with sounds of mayhem: cracking of wood, shattering of glass, and screams from those trying to survive the onslaught of the whirling debris.

And then it was silent. It was over just as quickly as it started. They lay there a few seconds before slowly lifting their heads and casting their eyes over the path of destruction.

"You okay?" the soldier asked.

"I'm fine," Emily nodded. "Uh...you can let us up now."

"Oh yes, sorry." He began to shimmy out from under the train. He looked over Emily intently. She was visibly shaken and confused.

"What are you looking at?" she questioned.

"Your head. That needs to get looked at. It's bleeding pretty good. You were knocked out cold when I ran by."

"Well, I feel fine. We're just fine. Swell."

"I'm sure you are. And what is your name?" he asked.

"I'm Duke, and this is Emily," she stated, her thoughts obviously clouded.

"You're Duke—and that is Emily?" he asked, second-guessing her statement, pointing back and forth between the two. "My name is John Markle."

"Hi, Duke. This is Emily, and I'm John," Emily said as she began to wobble on her one remaining shoe.

"Yep, all right, let's get you some help."

"I don't need any help, Duke!" Emily snapped as she bobbled forward and suddenly collapsed in his arms.

John gazed at her as she moaned lightly, pressing the palm of her hand against her forehead. Despite her crimson brow, she was stunningly beautiful. She opened her eyes and looked at him briefly, intently wondering who this young man was. Her dark locks of hair and big, brown, doe eyes stunned John and left him speechless. Tornado-ridden and all, she was the loveliest woman he had ever laid eyes on. Hers was the face he had always imagined when he closed his eyes at night, every night. He was drawn to her, though he didn't know her. She seemed strong and independent yet fragile and vulnerable. And he had just saved her life.

"Duke. Come here," he said, full of pride and shaking his head. "You're a damn good dog!"

Duke came and sat next to him while he held Emily. He knelt to the ground, allowing her limp body to rest back against his. He shook her lightly while charmingly repeating her name. Duke nudged her cheek with his wet nose as if doing his own check on her well-being. John noticed a leaf of folded paper fall from her pocket just as he spotted a medic rushing toward them in the distance. John quickly opened the paper containing Emily's information about Dogs for Defense. The creased parchment described a new program that would train civilian dogs and teach them to be soldiers, to save lives on the battlefield. The document proudly stated in bold letters that this program was the first of its kind and was led by one Lieutenant Brass. Emily was clearly a part of it—and instantly John wanted to be as well. He quickly folded the paper back up and slipped it into his pocket as the medic approached.

"Dear God. Is she all right?" he asked, out of breath.

"She needs a doctor. She knocked herself out, and she's been talking gibberish," John said, concerned.

"Let's get her over to the infirmary," said the seasoned gray-haired medic. "She's probably got a concussion."

The medic added impatiently, "What do you want to do with that dog? He can't come with us."

John squeezed the paper in his pocket and looked over at Duke. John replied to the medic, "The hell he can't. Where's the hospital? Let's go!"

"There's a clinic on the other side. We can take a shortcut and run between these two buildings," the medic said.

He led the way as John carried Emily. Duke stayed right by their side. John's mind was reeling back and forth. He always knew that he wanted to be a marine. Perhaps unknowingly, Emily had just steered him in a direction that he'd never considered. Perhaps Duke was leading him down a proverbial path that was meant specifically for him. Maybe Duke was just the vessel chosen by a higher power. Maybe his dear mother was stirring something inside him from heaven above. His mind was racing as they maneuvered through the buildings, making their way to the infirmary.

"Hey. Where can I find Lieutenant Brass?" John asked the medic.

"You can find him up at Camp Lejeune. Building four, most likely. Just look for the loud bald guy," the medic chuckled.

"Thanks," John said abruptly.

"What do you need with him, anyway?"

"Are we almost there?" John quickly changed the subject back to the task at hand.

They began to hustle faster down the hallways, making their way toward the double doors at the end. John was carrying Emily over his shoulders. He was amazed that Duke hadn't taken off yet. Most dogs would have tucked tail and run away, but Duke was sticking close by. John thought maybe the dog was just scared. Where else would he go? Even if Duke did wander off, he could certainly make it on his own. But Duke didn't want to leave the action. Duke wanted to hang around and be a part of it. It was as if he didn't want to miss out. Seemingly, loyalty to the soldier was already engrained in his Doberman soul. Suddenly he started barking at a door that was half-closed. The medic and John did not want to stop. They both believed the infirmary would be packed full of people looking for care and a doctor. Selfishness is situational, and in this situation it was well deserved. John put her well-being above everything else. She had woken up and opened her eyes a few times, trying to say a few things that were inaudible. At one point John was comforting her, telling her she would be okay, and Emily gazed at him and smiled.

"I must be in heaven," Emily said. "You...you must be an angel."

John smiled back and said, "You're about to be in the hospital, which is probably a better place, considering."

They finally got to the clinic, and the small, dark, waiting room was filled to capacity. The lady behind the counter would randomly call out a name, and several different people would respond. Everyone was looking for help. They were finally seen by a doctor about an hour later, and just as suspected, it was a concussion. The helpful medic made a small pallet on the floor beside Emily's bed for Duke, in order to comfort Emily, and he said his good-byes so he could attend to other people. The doctor wanted to keep Emily overnight, so John said his good-byes too. Maybe she heard them; maybe she didn't. John pulled the slip of paper once again from his pocket. He looked over at Duke and he realized why he'd stuck by their side the entire time. Emily had been training Duke and several other dogs prior to getting to North Carolina. Her scent still on his hands, John couldn't shake the thought of Emily. He knew his immediate task was to get to Camp Lejeune and find Lieutenant Brass.

5

CAMP LEJEUNE

John walked outside the clinic back into the devastated land. He began to realize how many buildings actually withstood the tornado. It looked like a war zone. He noticed an old Willys jeep close by with two marines climbing into it. He ran over and asked if they were going over to Camp Lejeune. The two older marines acknowledged and asked if he needed a ride. During casual conversation with the older marines, they indicated that the tornado had just missed Camp Lejeune. They sustained minimal damage, with only a few buildings suffering some minor damage.

North Carolina in 1943 was just pockmarked with small towns. Many of them were poor, with not too many wealthy or affluent individuals, especially in their area. Most of the work there was farming or agricultural, and the hot June sun damaged their crops just as the Great Depression damaged their small, local economy. These were strong people, a patriotic group located on the East Coast of the United States, and they were God-fearing. Many of the veterans of World War I lived in the area. After December 7, 1941, many of the younger men were eager to go defend their country. To do what their forefathers did to protect the United States from tyranny was an honor and a privilege. John wanted to think that Emily was the reason he wanted to be a marine but deep down inside he wanted to be a hero. After all, he had signed up before he even knew her. He concluded she was a guardian angel sent from his mother above to keep him safe. And she was beautiful. It was hard for John to discount that fact. He was going to have to convince Lieutenant Brass to let him be part of the war dog platoons.

Camp Lejeune was only a couple of years old and still in its infancy. Most of the foliage was tall pine trees and shady hardwoods. What wasn't covered in trees was covered with hills, farmland, wetlands, and marshland. There were some fields of corn still around in sporadic pockets.

The marines in the Willys dropped John off and went back into Jacksonville. The topography reminded him of home. He looked around for a little while and gazed over the hills. It was a pretty sight in the midday sun. The sun rays danced an inviting dance off the flowing water from the New River. His peaceful little daydream was abruptly stopped when he felt a large hand tapping on his right shoulder and a voice echo out asking if he was lost. He knew who it was without even having to turn around: Lieutenant Brass. This was confirmed when John turned around although Brass's overbearing voice didn't quite match his medium stature.

"You found what the hell it is you're looking for?" Lieutenant Brass squawked.

John immediately turned around and saluted. "Sir, yes sir. I believe I have."

Private Markle realized this was his chance, and he needed to go about it the right way. Chances are he'd only have one shot at it. He could tell just by looking at Brass's crinkled eyebrows and wrinkled forehead that he was a serious man and one of conviction.

"Well, what is it that you're looking for, Private?"

"Sir, I'm looking for you. I believe you're Lieutenant Brass."

Brass pointed at his jacket pocket and, with a combination of sarcasm and authority, said, "I'm glad to see you passed the seein' test. Now what is it that I can do for you, Private? We're kinda busy around here with the tornado and all."

"Sir, my name is Private John Markle. I am asking for assignment to the war dog platoons," he said, with as much confidence as he could.

He said it. Got it out of the way and out into the open. His question was now floating around in the mind of Lieutenant Brass. Judging by the stare on his face, John thought he may have even been contemplating it.

"Volunteering? And Private, what makes you qualified to be in my platoon? I'm not gonna go through the trouble if you're not qualified. Shit, son, I have soldiers lining up to be a part of this." Lieutenant Brass leaned in and continued, "Why you?"

John, feeling a little bit intimidated now, said, "Sir, I grew up on a farm in Little Rock. There were horses. There were dogs. We even had pigs and chickens. I took care of them all, especially those chickens. They were good, and the bacon, thick-sliced."

Brass interrupted and said, "All right, son, I don't need your life story. Tell me, what kind of dogs did you have on your farm?"

He thought before he responded. This was the make-or-break question, and it was time to lay it on thick.

"Well, sir, we had a couple of mutts—" John said as he thought about Duke.

"Mutts?"

John sensed Lieutenant Brass pulling back and quickly added, "—and a couple Dobermans."

John had a knack for reading people. He knew he had Brass's attention now, and he wasn't one to tell lies, but he thought he and God would just need to settle this one later. This was just a little white lie, no more harmful than telling children about Santa Claus at

Christmas. It was for a good cause, and nobody would get hurt.

"Tell you what, Private Markle, I'll see what I can do."

"Sir, thank you, sir."

"Is there something you need to be doing right now?" Brass questioned.

"Sir, yes sir, I'm on my way to help. And Lieutenant, can I make a request?"

"Another?" grumbled Brass.

"Sir, I request to be assigned to Duke. He's one of those Dogs for Defense donated dogs."

Lieutenant Brass cocked his head and squinted back at John, contemplating whether or not to ask how he came to know one of the donated dogs. Things were a little too hectic for him to even worry about that, so he passed on the opportunity. Much to the relief of John, Brass just stared and quickly turned around, walking off in the other direction. John was left wondering if that was an acknowledgment of his request or if he had overstepped his boundaries by asking for Duke.

John was elated to get his assignment papers a few days later. He thought to himself that he really didn't know what he was doing, but then again, did any of these other young men? It was extremely busy that morning at the training camp. The dogs were being unloaded and brought one by one into the veterinarian's office, who just happened to be Lieutenant Brass.

"Bring him over here," ordered Lieutenant Brass.

Gunnery Sergeant Tomahawk grabbed Duke and set him up on the table. Tomahawk, a middle-aged Native American with tan weathered skin, was eager to help.

"Good boy. Let's see those teeth. Smile for us," he said.

Duke gave Lieutenant Brass a big lick on his right cheek showing his affection to his new leader of the war dog platoons.

"Good boy. You'll do just fine," Brass said with a smile as he lifted him down and walked him over to the scale. "Duke, eighty-five pounds!" He had to yell over the barking of the other dogs, so that his assistant could jot it down.

Tomahawk picked Duke up and sat him back on the table while two other marines came over and held him still, pulling back his cropped ear. The sound of the tattoo needle caused Duke to perk up and look around. There was a lot of commotion in the office, and Duke seemed to take to it quite well, but something about that tattoo needle just didn't sit well with him. It made him nervous. The two other marines held him tight while Tomahawk tattooed Duke's enlistment number on the inside of his ear.

Lieutenant Brass yelled out, "Duke A089!"

Duke was now a marine.

The next day at training camp, which was located right by a little peninsula of the New River, was a big day. Everyone was gathered around, lined up at attention and listening to Lieutenant Brass.

"Quiet down! When I call your name, step forward. Private Gregory! Step forward and move to the right." Private Gregory was a well-built, muscular young man. He towered over the other young privates. His massive six-foot-six-inch frame was hard to miss and demanded respect.

Lieutenant Brass continued to bark out orders. When he called out John's name, John stepped forward, landing his right foot in a pile of fresh dog crap. A few of his comrades laughed as he scraped it from his shoe.

"Watch your step," remarked Private O'Ryan with a smart-ass tone.

Lieutenant Brass continued to pace the line of young recruits in order to ensure they were aware of his presence and authority. He let everybody know quickly that their shenanigans would not be tolerated, and if anyone wanted to test that theory they would be cleaning shit from the kennels for the next week.

"All right, ladies. Today I'm gonna assign you your dog. This dog is the key to your survival. Many lives depend on this animal. This dog will love you unconditionally. I, however, already hate all of you. You will earn my respect. Anyone who harms a dog with physical discipline will be dealt with severely. Your dog will always outrank you. You keep this animal happy. A happy dog will save your life. It will save other people's lives. Keep this dog happier than your wife, your girl-friend, and your boyfriends. Got it?"

Marines responded in unison, "Yes, sir!"

Lieutenant Brass continued, "Good! Now, when I call your name, step up and get your paperwork. This paperwork contains all the information you will need to know about your dog. Learn it. Live it. Know it. You will know everything about your dog. Private Gregory, you're assigned Fever A096."

Gregory stepped up and grabbed his paperwork and immediately fell back in line.

"Private Shit Shoe. You're assigned Duke A089."

Private Markle did not realize that Lieutenant Brass was referring to him.

"Private Markle! Step your ass forward, son!" snapped Lieutenant Brass. "Did you take that shit from your shoe and stuff it into your ears?"

"No, sir!" replied John.

"That's good! I would really be worried about you if you were stuffing shit in your ears. Step back in line," Lieutenant Brass said with a smile on his face.

At this point John couldn't tell if Brass didn't like him or if he was just busting his balls. John wondered if he was going to make his life a miserable hell and make him pay for requesting to be moved to his platoons. Maybe Lieutenant Brass knew what was motivating John.

He got little reassurance when Private O'Ryan laughed out loud. Lieutenant Brass did not take kindly to his laughter and ordered him on kennel duty for the next two days. O'Ryan noticed John and a few others smiling. John grabbed his nose, pinching it and waved his hand in front of his face as if he were fanning the air in front of him.

The men spent that night in their barracks, comparing the paperwork for their dogs. Brass had made it clear they were to know anything and everything about their new companion. He went on to compare the dogs to their issued rifles. They both could be deadly weapons, silent when needed and loud and ferocious when warranted. The marines were curious and eager to get to know their dogs and see what they were capable of. A majority of them were assigned dogs that were donated by patriotic families or families that had come upon hard times. How a donated dog from a domestic household could handle the tension and stress of battle would remain to be seen. That was a topic of debate between them.

"I got a Shepherd named Titan. One and a half years old and really high marks on his DFD report. Maybe I lucked out," Rumery said. "Look at this picture."

The picture submitted by the donated family showed Titan rearing his teeth, his gums extracted up the side of his snout. It was a menacing pose.

Gregory chimed in. "I have a Doberman named Fever. Looks like he actually did time at Bougainville. He's a killer."

Private Smiles indicated he had a Doberman named Blade. Smiles had a smile on his face, as always, with his grin nearly reaching the rim of his large eyeglasses.

Private Markle opened his paperwork, and a letter from Tommy Johnson hit the floor. Curious, he picked it up and concealed it in his pocket.

"I've got a Doberman named Duke. Donated from the Johnson family from Illinois. I wonder how these dogs are going to fare in war? How well did DFD train them and get them ready for our training? Volunteer dogs." John questioned the validity of the program with his tone.

"How can a dog volunteer?" asked Rumery.

"The family decides. I don't know," John replied.

"So some little old lady donates her fucking poodle for service?" Rumery changed his voice upward and continued, "Here, little Japs. Be scared of my big, bad, fluffy poodle! He's coming to get you in the jungle!"

"Stop being an asshole." Gregory said, butting in.

Private O'Ryan walked over to their area and joined them.

"What did you say?" Rumery responded as he took a stand.

"I said queers can't hear," replied Gregory.

Rumery, growing angry, replied, "Stand up! I'll show you queer, Texas boy."

"Looks like I came over at the right time," O'Ryan said.

Gregory took to his feet, towering over the little Italian Rumery. A few marines were egging them on, hoping to see a fight. O'Ryan was standing now, inciting the potential for the two marines to clash with one another.

"Shut it, O'Ryan," John said. "No need for us to fight among ourselves."

"Fuck off, Markle."

"You have a problem with me, asshole? We can settle it any time you want. I'm not going anywhere anytime soon." John stood up.

They were all arguing now: John with O'Ryan, and Rumery pressing his luck with Gregory. The tension in the room elevated.

"You talk a lot of shit for someone smaller than my turds," Gregory said as he looked down on Rumery.

He replied, "So what are you going to do about it?"

Gregory clenched his fists. "You want me to show you how we do things in Texas? You want that, Howdy Doodie? I will fold you up like a pretzel and make you cry for momma."

Gregory reached out to grab Rumery's neck, but John jumped in the middle, trying to be a peacemaker.

"Whoa, big guy."

"I'm gonna crush his little pea head!"

Rumery avoided the oversized grasp and retreated to the opposite side of the room as he saw Lieutenant Brass enter the barracks.

They all got to attention in his presence.

"What the hell is going on in here?" yelled Brass. "Am I going to have to ask again? Private Markle! Private Markle, what the hell is going on in here?"

"Sir, a simple disagreement. That's all."

"A simple disagreement? Private Markle, do I look like a fathead to you? Do I?" Brass was still yelling at the top of his voice.

"No, sir!"

"Why in God's name is Rumery hiding over there?" asked Brass.

Rumery, trying to protect his honor, responded from the other side of the room. "Sir, I'm not hiding—"

Cutting him off quickly, Brass told him to shut his mouth and responded to John.

"Sir, there was confusion over the Dogs for Defense program and the War Dog program, sir. That'll all," John said.

Brass circled the room, giving everyone the stink eye. Little did they know he had been listening to them from the start of their conversation. He could tell these young men would make great marines, most of them at least. They were feisty and had fire in their bellies. He was a bit worried. He had seen the atrocities of war put out those fires. He thought if these young men could hold it together, bond with each other and their four-legged companions, then they should be fine.

He finished circling the room and made his way back to Gregory.

He whispered to him, "Son, you crush his pea head if he ever puts down Texas again." He turned to walk out of the room.

"I know everything! I see everything! I hear everything! Get some sleep, pansies."

Everyone sighed as he walked out.

6

TRAINING

"**Y**ou think we can get these young men in line and ready?" Brass asked as he peered out the window of his tiny office.

Tomahawk responded, "Sir, they can be whipped into shape. I believe the bigger question is how motivated are they. Most of them probably feel like they got assigned to some nonsense program."

"Private Markle volunteered. He tracked me down and asked for a transfer."

They continued to talk back and forth, knowing they faced an uphill battle to win the respect of their fellow soldiers.

"We can cure those thoughts. These marines and their dogs will make history. Shit, they'll become heroes to be honored for decades to come," preached Brass. "When we're finished, I wouldn't wanna be on the other end of one of these dogs. We'll have everyone whistling a different tune."

It was good to hear the confidence in his voice. He stood tall, looking out the window. Tomahawk straightened up and reciprocated the tone.

"Yes, sir," he replied.

"Speaking of tunes, get Smiles a real bugle. It sounds like he's playing a damn kazoo every morning."

Smiles woke the marines up every morning with that bugle call. He got better over time, but this particular morning it sounded like he was blowing in the wrong end. John and the others ran past him as the hurried out of the barracks and over to where Brass was standing.

"Dear God. Who taught you to play that thing?" questioned John.

"I learned in school."

"You didn't learn anything," he replied as he ran past. Typical banter for these two. John always gave him a hard time, but they valued each other's friendship.

Everyone made their way over to Lieutenant Brass, where he proceeded to tell them about the dogs he was going to assign them. He covered the basic material and emphasized that a dog was issued property, a loaded weapon to be treated with respect, and the dog would always outrank its handler. This was to ensure that any physical harm against an animal would be treated as if the harm were against a higher ranking officer. He explained how all the dogs had been inspected and trained by Dogs for Defense. They examined each dog for aggressiveness, responsiveness, temperament, shell shock, and overall physical ability.

"These are the best the United States has to offer," Brass concluded before assigning a dog to each marine.

Private Markle was excited to see Duke once again, so when Brass yelled his name and told him to go find Duke's crate, he took off in a full sprint. John's action, or his reaction, brought a rare smile to Brass's otherwise stern demeanor. He watched as John opened the crate. Duke immediately licked John's face as he affectionately rubbed the canine's head and ears.

After all of them were assigned their dogs, all except Ricci, out walked a lonely-looking poodle.

"Private Ricci, meet your dog, Fluffy!" Brass yelled.

The group erupted in laughter, and Gregory couldn't resist throwing a verbal jab at Ricci. He and Fever stood a few feet away.

"Don't take that dog to Texas," he whispered to Ricci.

Ricci couldn't stand it. The little Italian's blood pressure shot up, and he rushed Gregory, bringing the small giant down to the dusty ground. What happened next surprised everyone. Fever, who had just met his handler, leaped on Ricci and reared his teeth, protecting his new companion. He placed his massive paws on each side of Ricci's head and lifted his lips, making sure he understood the dominant position he had on him.

"Holy shit! Fever! Out! Out!" Brass screamed.

Fever backed off and sat down. He then glanced over at Fluffy the poodle, showed his teeth, and turned back around. Everyone was quite impressed with Fever's reaction.

"You see, ladies! That's loyalty! Whoooo weeeee! Get off the ground, for God's sake, soldier! Show some dignity!" Brass yelled as he bent over Ricci and offered him a hand. That was one thing about the Lieutenant, he always made sure his marines knew he was in charge, but he also made sure they knew he was one of them.

The majority of the dogs were well behaved, indicative of the training first bestowed upon them by Emily and the Dogs for Defense program. There were some, such as Colt, a German shepherd with a full black snout, that were a bit on the antisocial side. Colt was handled by Carlos Cammacho. He had a cousin who was born in Guam and still resided there, at least up until the Japanese invasion. He hadn't heard from him in years—many years. Last he'd heard, he was attending night class at a high school and selling fish door to door. Carlos had a personal battle to go along with his marine duties. He and Colt both had personal battles, it seemed.

Colt sat barking for no apparent reason as the marines and their dogs gathered around Brass to get some instructions. They had spent the day training with their dogs, and Brass instructed them to break out and find some quiet time with their four-legged companions.

"You will spend the next few days getting to know your dog, his mannerisms, his likes, and his dislikes— what makes him tick. Study what his alert is, men. It may be as simple as twisting an ear or throwing his nose in the air. It may be as blunt as a full-on point, front leg lifted and all. Get to know him. He is studying you as well. Make a friend," Lieutenant Brass said.

The barking from Colt had turned to Duke, but Duke paid it no attention. He sat there, curious and alert, like the studious kid that sits in the front row of ninth-grade math class. Brass had to eventually tell Cammacho to get his dog under control. It wasn't too late to get a dog removed from the program. In fact, a few had already been sent back for various reasons, but the common theme they shared was over aggressiveness. Dogs with that character flaw didn't last very long. It's not that Colt was very aggressive but he was very loud.

Brass assured Cammacho that if he didn't get the barking under control he was gone. "Instead of saving lives, he just gave up our position and got us all killed, Cammacho!"

Duke and John broke away from the group and sat at the elevated edge of the riverbank, facing a glowing, reddish-orange sunset. Gregory, O'Ryan, Ricci, and Smiles all sat within a fifty-foot-diameter circle of one another. Despite their earlier shortcomings, they all seemed to like each other. Being a handler made them feel part of an elite group, a group to be reckoned with. However, they all wanted their personal space to befriend their new companion and fellow marine. They respected each other's privacy during these special moments.

John pulled a letter from his herringbone-twill pants and read it aloud to Duke. Little Tommy Johnson had addressed the letter to Duke, not Private John Markle. While some people may have thought that was odd, John knew the young boy's intentions. He was writing to his best friend, not the people who took his best friend away. His words were simple and to the point. He missed his friend and hoped he was doing well. He told Duke his parents had moved into the apartment, and his room was really small. He went on to say that his mother, Sherry, had found a job working four or five days a week at a local diner. Ty was still looking. They all missed their beloved Duke and hoped for his safe return. His parents wrote that at the bottom of the letter.

Duke just stared into the distant sun, watching it slowly disappear from view until John said one word that grabbed his attention. Squirrels. One word mentioned in Tommy's letter caused Duke to perk up and tilt his head in curiosity. He said it again. Squirrels.

"What dog doesn't like to chase squirrels?" John said to his new buddy.

Duke responded by scooting a little closer, now leaning on his new buddy. Everything seemed to fade away like the sun, casting growing shadows as the sunlight gave way to the night sky. Duke turned his pointed snout and licked John on his face.

"That little boy sure loves you," John said as he gave him a pat on the head.

They spent the next few days working with their dogs on various activities: sentry, messaging, and scouting. These were daily training activities the marines would conduct until deployment. The attack training was the favorite of Lieutenant Brass. The amount of protection the makeshift bite suit provided was questionable. Used rubber tires lined the inside of a padded cloth arm-guard. Several guys, including Gregory and O'Ryan, discovered the suit's imperfections a few times, resulting in bite marks.

John was excited to see Emily again. They were working with Duke, practicing hand signals as he ran through some basic obstacles. This test was designed to test the dogs' ability to see signals from afar and obey. No words were used. The ability to control the dog from a distance was critical to success and to protect the men.

John was attracted to Emily but he was unsure if it was mutual. She smiled a lot and made people feel at ease. She would shyly look away as he flirted, but she soon reciprocated the playful banter. She was glowing, as she always was, and he was covered in dust and dirt from the attack training earlier.

"Good boy, Duke. He's a quick learner," she said.

"He's fast, smart, strong, and dedicated," John remarked as he signaled for Duke to sit. Duke was twenty yards away and obeyed.

"That's how I like my dogs."

John smiled and replied, "And your men?"

"Slow, dumb, and dishonorable," she said with sarcasm.

"I see. Maybe you should stick with dogs."

"Maybe I should."

They both laughed and shyly broke eye contact. John was at ease with her remarks, and she was comfortable with him. Emily continued to explain how she'd gotten involved with the program. They had a lot to talk about that day. She told him how her first love was horses, but when the dogs came around she knew she wanted to be a part of the War Dog program. She had trained Duke from the day he arrived. She knew he was special. She knew all the dogs were special, but Duke always seemed to be one notch above the others. His speed and his agility were steps above the rest. Fever, Raptor, Titan, and Blade were exceptional dogs, but Duke always seemed to rise above. Some of the guys would call him and John show-offs.

John shared with her his mother's love for horses and her positive outlook on life in general. He shared with her the death of his mother and the effects that bulbar polio had had on her life and their family's life. It was painful to watch the disease take his mother's mobility away. Her breathing was stressed, and she had trouble conducting simple activities. It eventually took her away from her horses. John and his dad would wheel her down to them, so she could watch her horses run in the fields. She taught John about death. She taught John about love and loss and how you should always cherish moments with those you love. Even the bad memories were just that: memories. Sometimes those bad memories stuck with you for life, pushing the good memories to the side. She stressed to John to not allow bad memories to curdle his view on life, because life's silver linings would even come in bad situations. You just had to know where to look to find them. She passed the day after she shared this with him.

Emily liked her new friend's openness. Not many people would share such a story, and she found John's sincerity uplifting and honest.

John finished the conversation by saying, "I knew I wanted to be a marine, to serve my country. Both Mom and Dad instilled that belief in me. She always said that when you do good things, great thing can happen to you. So here I am, and here you are. And here's this guy." He pointed to Duke.

"Coincidence?" she asked.

"I have to confess," he said, as he pulled her lost Dogs for Defense papers from his pocket, "I asked for a transfer to the War Dog program when I found this the day of the tornado."

Emily was quite flattered and said so. She playfully asked, "And how do you know I'm available, Private John Markle?"

"I don't, but maybe you're my silver lining in this war." He grabbed her hand and smiled.

She returned the smile.

They were unaware they were being watched by O'Ryan as he and Ricci cleaned out the kennels, just as Brass ordered.

"And once we're through here, we'll be shipped over to some Godforsaken island. The Japs are embedded over there. Foxholes, pillboxes, booby traps. All kinds of shit happening over there. If they can't shoot you, they'll fuckin' stab you. I've heard stories about them hanging our soldiers by their own intestines. Shit, those little sonsabitches carry swords," O'Ryan said as he peered over the fence, watching the two make sweet with each other.

Ricci replied, "I'm not scared."

"Enemy fire isn't the only fire to watch out for, if you know what I mean." O'Ryan tossed a large shovel of shit over his shoulder as his jealousy began to fester.

Some of the best training exercises were the mock beach landings. The Higgins boats would cut through the choppy water, splashing the salty Atlantic water in their faces, cooling them down. Gregory and Ricci were still nipping at each other, neither one willing to let go of the fight from a few days before.

When the gate dropped, Duke was first out, not waiting for it to fully deploy, and he led the way. This day, Gregory and Ricci became entangled in their dogs' leashes as Fever and Titan crossed paths, throwing them to the sand. Lieutenant Brass yelled at everyone to keep their heads down, keep their helmets on, and haul ass—or they wouldn't make it come real combat.

The dogs seemed to know this without being told. Despite being accustomed to gunfire and explosions, the dogs still jumped and pulled at their leashes as the sand and ground was thrown into the air beside them.

"What are you two lovebirds doing? Get off your asses and get to running! You'll get yourself killed out there!" Brass yelled.

"I'm six foot five. It's hard to keep my head down," Gregory said under his breath.

Everyone knew these mock landings would be invaluable in the near future. John and Duke ran over to help them up.

I love the smell of gun powder!" John yelled, and he reached down to lend a hand. "Get up! Let's go!"

The young marines had had their dogs for a few weeks now. Training had been going well, and progress was obvious, for both the men and their dogs. They sat around one evening, and Brass decided to test them to see what they had learned of and from their companions since they'd met. He started off with Fever, bragging over his display of loyalty and protective qualities and asked Gregory what he had learned from him.

"Sir, Fever is a loyal dog. He is aggressive and displays all the qualities we need to accomplish our mission," Gregory said.

"And Smiles, what have you learned about Blade?" questioned Brass.

"Sir, Blade has one hell of a nose. He has excelled at detecting hidden dangers and locating the enemy's scent."

"Son, have you learned to play that damn bugle any better?"

"Somewhat, sir!" Smiles replied, careful not to incriminate himself. He had been practicing but not improving much.

Everyone else responded aptly to the pleasure of Brass. He congratulated his men on their progress but reminded them they had a long way to go. He reminded them they would be shipping out in a month's time, although he wouldn't elaborate more on where. John and his group assumed it would be Camp Pendleton and then off to the Pacific, an assumption that would prove true and completely change the scope of the war—and their lives.

"Private Markle, tell me some more about Duke," Brass asked.

John proceeded to tell the group about Tommy Johnson and the letters he had been writing to Duke. These letters, literally addressed to Duke, were coming in every other day. Some were long and some were short, but they all asked that he make it home safe and to keep the marines out of harm's way.

"And he writes these letters to Duke? Private Markle, does the dog write back?" Brass asked sarcastically.

"Yes, sir, Duke has excellent handwriting," John joked.

"A bunch of jokers today, huh?" asked Brass. "Well, all right, get the dogs put up. And for heaven's sake, marine, get Colt under control."

Colt sat barking at Duke, who was paying him no attention. Somehow he got satisfaction from snubbing the overactive shepherd. It seemed he never passed up the opportunity to make Colt look crazy.

But maybe crazy was the normal for these dogs and these marines. The training surely made them more aggressive and determined. Going from a farm or a nice house with a nice family and then being thrown into war dog training had its effects, even more for the dogs than the soldiers, although John, Gregory, and rest of the bunch knew what they were getting into. The war had been going on for years. They had seen the pictures and heard on the radio. They had witnessed heroes of the war but knew not of the actions they'd committed to obtain that medal, that Silver Star, or that Purple Heart. Every single one of those honors came with a heavy price: a lost friend, a lost limb, a lost life. The worst loss of all wasn't a wound, or at least not a physical one. Emotionally, they earned those honors every day long after their enlistment. John, Gregory, Ricci, Smiles, and O'Ryan all shared something; every soldier shares something. That's patriotism. They all loved their country. That's why they were there. But the dogs—they had no idea. They had the internal desire to guard and to protect, and to harm whoever they were told to. They certainly did not choose to be there, but they accepted it every day and woke up every morning willing to do it all over.

Their reason was simple: to please their handler, their master, and their companion. Their intentions were ever so clear during training. To them it was all a game. There wasn't a difference between live-fire training and real combat in their minds. It was one and the same.

The group typically conducted live-fire training close to the river, but on one occasion they were training farther into the natural landscape. The dense, overgrown trees kept the smoke from escaping into the grasp of the blue sky. A blast would sometimes quickly lift the tree limbs and allow the sun to cast smoky shadows along the terrain. The heat from the explosion would rapidly dissipate, causing the limbs to retract, closing the eye to the sky.

Duke and John were running through the woods, John firing his sidearm rapidly into the air as he yelled.

Duke was off his leash during this exercise. Most of the dogs at this point in training could be controlled without a leash, but live fire was always a test. It tested the dogs' judgment under pressure every time. Many times a dog just took off and ran in the opposite direction, away from the noise and commotion. Some struggled with the decision to either tuck tail or to stay and fulfill their duties as marines. In the beginning of training, half the group struggled with those instincts—God-given instincts. Three weeks into training, their rookie precognitions had gone by the wayside, and they would all stand their ground next to their handlers.

Duke raised his nose in the air, flexing his thick, black nostrils as his brain calculated and separated the hundreds of different scents. From the smoke appeared O'Ryan and Raptor, walking in his direction, pistols in hand. They did not break eye contact as he approached.

"What do you want, O'Ryan?"

"I've been looking for you. You need to understand something. I'll say it once because I know you're a slow plowboy: Emily."

John placed the leash back on Duke and replied, "What about her?"

"Stay away from her."

"What did you say?"

"You heard me. Emily. Stay away from her. She's not here for you. She's here for me." O'Ryan stepped into John.

"Understand?"

"Fuck off, O'Ryan. You know, I don't care where you came from or what brought your ugly ass here, but you can go to hell."

John stepped back as a nearby explosion tossed dirt and debris all around them. The dirt flew into O'Ryan's face, and his sweat washed it onto his lips. He moved his cigar from one corner of his mouth to the other and spat, being sure to aim at John's boots.

"You're gonna mess around and get yourself killed out there. Watch yourself." He and Raptor turned and were slowly absorbed by the forest and smoke. Gregory came running up, his bulging biceps bleeding through his torn sleeve.

"What was that all about?"

"I'll tell you later," John replied. "What the hell is that?" He pointed at the wound.

"I fell. Cut it on a fallen tree limb." Gregory's ability to tell a lie was subpar at best. His big white teeth somehow made his fib even less believable. John knew he and Fever had been roughhousing. Fever, sometimes short on temper and patience, resorted to going after his arm, mimicking the attack drills. That dog was loyal but damn unpredictable at times.

The following morning the group was running the obstacle course with their dogs. They were always with their dogs, and as the time to leave crept closer, first by the day and now nearly by the hour, the young marines grew anxious. Some hoped the stories they'd heard weren't real and that their participation in the war would be limited. Others, however, longed for the day they could inflict injury on the opposition. Those were driven by the stories they'd heard, and they silently kept their anger inside while others were vocal about their future intentions and would brag about what they were going to do. John was a realist and knew the dangers, and he knew the stories were true.

"It's kill or be killed, right?" he asked Gregory.

"Shoot first. Ask questions later," Smiles chimed in.

They were running alongside each other on the course, carrying on the conversation. Duke clawed and climbed his way to the top of the ten-foot fence, where he sat overlooking the course.

Gregory replied, "I'm gonna kill one of those bastards and bring his sword back with me. Pass it down to my kids."

John glanced over and caught Emily watching them from across the field. They both enjoyed locking eyes. It felt natural to them.

Gregory noticed and said, "Oh, that's what it's about."

"What what's about?" John asked.

"That girl over there. I've been noticing how friendly you two are to each other."

"What? No." John tried to conceal his feelings.

"Don't bullshit us, Markle. Come on, that asshole O'Ryan looks to be sweet on her too."

"Yeah. Look." Smiles pointed to O'Ryan as he walked up to her.

"Yes, we've talked a few times."

"Look at the gams on her. I'm not mad at ya, Markle," Smiles said. "Shit, I think I may be jealous."

They watched from a distance as O'Ryan threw his hands in the air and moved them around as if he were giving a speech. His actions appeared frustrated, but they could only see the conversation, not hear it. Emily put her head down, avoiding eye contact with O'Ryan. After a minute or so, he spit out his cigar and turned and walked away. Emily looked over at John and gave an awkward smile and half-empty wave. She was embarrassed that he'd witnessed the conversation. John was struggling with O'Ryan and his actions as of late. He could deal with O'Ryan and his overall bad attitude within their group, but his connection with Emily was stronger than his patience for O'Ryan.

John rubbed the birthmark on his left forearm. He sometimes did that when he was bothered by something. It kept him grounded. He equated his birthmark with his life and the things he had experienced in his eighteen short years. It kept him connected with his past while building his character for the future. Everything happened for a reason, and within that reason was a lesson, a life lesson that most people unknowingly learned and stuck back in their subconscious, only to be recalled at a later date.

They were leaving in a few days. John didn't have time to worry about O'Ryan and his shenanigans. His concern was Emily.

7

CROSS-COUNTRY

The announcement was made that they were heading to Camp Pendleton in California in two days. The marines were glad to leave the North Carolina heat, especially since it was the middle of July. They were to go there and complete training with the paratroopers and raiders. They all assumed they would eventually head to the Pacific.

They held a huge press event where they could showcase their dogs. There were exhibits of their training and live exercises. Everyone wanted their picture with a "devil dog." The reporters and photographers were having a ball with this event.

One reporter yelled for John and Duke to pose for a photo. John took a knee and Duke sat next to him. Duke licked John's face just as the flashbulb lit the sky.

"Thank you, young man," said the elderly reporter.

"My pleasure," John replied. "Can you send that photo to this address, please?" He handed him Tommy's name and address. "This dog was donated by this little boy and his family," John explained.

"Yes, I will, but these pictures are going national, young man. You're going to be seen all around the country. These dogs are heroes already," the reporter said.

"Well, if that's the case then get us all in a picture!"

Gregory, Ricci, Smiles, and even O'Ryan jumped at the opportunity for fame and cracked huge smiles as they jockeyed for the best position in the shot. Then they all broke away from each other and were embracing this media spectacle. John looked around for Emily and after a few seconds spotted her across the courtyard. He rushed over to her side.

"Oh, hi there," she said playfully.

"Hi. I saw you from over there."

"I saw you from over here."

"I wanted to say hi," he said.

"You already did that, Private."

Their playful conversation was effortless. They knew there was a connection between them.

John replied, "Yes, Yes, I did. I recall that. I saw you talking to—"

Emily interrupted him. "You're leaving tomorrow, John. I heard. That's why the media is here."

"They love us," he said. "I want to see you more before I go."

"Me too."

"I saw you talking to O'Ryan a few days ago." He posed his question as a statement. "Are you friends?"

"Friends?" She laughed. "That's funny. He can be an asshole, huh?"

"I didn't know I was falling for a sailor," he said, referring to her use of a curse word.

"Did he say something to you?"

"I reckon," said John. "It was really awkward but he showed up in the middle of a live fire and just—"

Gregory yelled from across the way, "Markle! Get over here! Here comes Brass!"

"Don't be late, Private," Emily said, with a flirty look in her eyes.

"I need to see you tonight!" he yelled as he ran away.

Emily's heart was fluttering. He made her feel special.

Later, after dinner, John and Duke went on sentry patrol. Smiles and Blade accompanied them. It was nice to be out at night with just you and your dog. Many of the guys enjoyed this assignment—at least doing it on base. It was a time to relax.

"Do you ever wonder about the stars? You know, like where they came from?" asked Smiles.

"I think the sky is heaven, and the stars are those who have lived a good life, passed on, and now sit up there with God," John responded.

"Whoa. That's an interesting philosophy," Smiles said as he stood up. "I'm gonna take a leak."

John walked behind the wooden fence and quickly penned a note to Emily, attached it to Duke's pouch, and sent him on his way. He hoped Duke knew where to go. He didn't want to get caught over by her housing, but he could explain it away if Duke was caught.

"All right, Duke. To Emily's. Go. Go," he ordered.

Duke took off in the wrong direction but quickly corrected and came running past John a few seconds later.

Duke made his way to Emily's door and began scratching and pawing at it, until she came to the door. She cautiously opened it and saw Duke sitting there. Surprised by his appearance at her door, she looked around, hoping to see John. She bent down to retrieve the letter in the pouch.

It was John's plea for her to meet him at midnight behind one of the buildings. It was a place that he and Duke would sometimes go to get away. She looked down at her watch and smiled.

"Good boy, Duke."

Duke turned and ran, disappearing into the shadows of the trees and buildings.

Emily arrived a bit out of breath from the midnight run. The moon lit her way through the East Coast night sky. She looked around for John. He and Duke suddenly appeared from the brush line, camouflaged by the shrubbery and shadows.

"Were you hiding in there?" she asked.

"We sometimes come out here at night. Duke likes it. It makes him feel at ease."

Duke was prancing around.

"He looks happy," she said.

"It's all a game to him," John said. "Everything is real, but nothing is real. You know?"

Emily leaned in and said, "Thanks for inviting me to your secret hideout."

They kissed passionately while embracing each other under the glow of the moon and stars. They had been anticipating this moment for some time.

"That was everything I thought it was going to be," he said.

"So you knew that was coming?"

"I'd hoped for it. And thought about it. A lot."

"Me too," she admitted as they continued to hold each other. "Um, what's that in your pocket, Private?"

He pulled out a small cigar box full of letters.

"These are from Tommy to Duke—and me, kind of," he said. "I want to make sure these stay safe. I could lose them out there."

"Of course, John," she said.

"Can I ask a favor too?"

"Depends," said Emily.

"Can you make sure they fix the War Dog sign? It doesn't even look like a dog."

He was referring to a sign in which the dog painted on it looked to be a cross between a Doberman and a great Dane.

"That's the favor? You can't think of anything better than that?" she joked.

"Another kiss?"

"A thousand more," she said.

She pulled out of their kiss after few seconds and reached behind her neck.

"Take this," she said. It was a locket with her picture in it, the silver slightly tarnished with age.

"I can't wait to give it back to you," he said honestly. "I'm scared."

"I'm scared for you, John."

They spent the rest of that night in each other's arms under the romantic glow of the night sky. Their love for each other blossomed that night, and their lives collided with reckless abandon.

The following day a huge parade was underway at the base. There was music from the all-black band from Montford Point on stage. Their jazzy sound filled the air with electricity and energy. Many families were in attendance, saying good-bye to their loved ones and seeing them off. Reporters were running around, talking with anyone who would talk back, their flashbulbs lighting up the morning sky as they documented the farewell.

John, Smiles, Gregory, Ricci, and O'Ryan stood off to the right of the stage. Smiles, trying to tell a joke, was cut off as Brass walked up.

"What are ya'll over here jawin' about?" he asked. "Never mind, I don't care. Smiles, you've been practicing, right?"

"A little, sir."

"A little, huh? Go borrow the band's bugle and play for our guests," Brass demanded.

"But sir," Smiles tried to explain.

"I don't care if he's a Negro, son. He fights for this country just like you and me." Brass stepped closer as he responded.

Smiles headed that way, cussing under his breath the entire way.

Brass questioned the remaining group as to how much Smiles had improved. Each gave mixed responses to his inquiry as they looked around at each other.

Smiles walked up on stage and motioned for the bugle. The black soldier holding it just smiled at him. He knew by his demeanor that Smiles was uncomfortable with the situation, and he decided to make it worse by purposely licking the mouthpiece. The trail of white foamy spit stretched from the mouthpiece to his tongue, creating a bridge of saliva. He did this in such a way that he made sure Smiles saw him.

This black man's spit, while troublesome to him, was not the end-all. Smiles was on a mission: to impress Lieutenant Brass. He grabbed the bugle, smiled his trademark smile, looked him straight in the eye, and then put that mouthpiece in his mouth. He didn't wipe it on his shirt or anything. He blew in it, creating a few obnoxious sounds. Brass heard the bugle from the side and shook his head, preparing for the worst.

Smiles turned to the crowd as he grabbed the microphone and said, "My friends call me Smiles, and I'm gonna play a song for you today."

The crowd erupted. Smiles turned to the band and asked if they knew "Boogie Woogie Bugle Boy." They obliged, and suddenly he was a different person. Most people got stage fright, but this side of Smiles was new to everyone. He was taken away by the energy from the crowd.

"Follow my lead," he said. "Ladies, you know what to do."

The three black ladies in the band shook their heads happily in agreement. "This isn't our first rodeo, Private," one responded. "You just play that bugle."

He put the bugle up to his lips and began by playing a flawless version of the Assembly bugle call. The crowd once again erupted in applause and cheers. His friends and Brass looked on in amazement. They had heard him butcher simple bugle calls like Reveille, First Sergeant's Call, and everyone's least favorite, First Call.

And with that he began the song solo, and then the band joined in and so did the three ladies. It was evident that they were seasoned professionals. This was a crowd favorite, and they'd obviously played it many, many times before.

"Can you believe this?" John asked.

Brass responded, "I thought I knew this kid." He walked away, and they all ran to the front of the stage to join in the fun.

John couldn't stop thinking about Emily. He looked around for her, but all the people created a wall, skewing his line of sight. Suddenly, she appeared from behind a large pole. John ran over to see her.

He was stopped by a group of black soldiers from Montford Point.

One of them asked, "Your friend always play the bugle like that? Where'd he learn to play like that?"

"No. That's remarkable, though," John replied, wondering if he really learned that in school.

"That boy's good."

They introduced each other as John looked over in Emily's direction. They explained they were from Montford Point and were trained to handle dogs too. Comically, they explained to John that despite the rumors, not all black people are scared of dogs. They all laughed and, paying no mind to segregation, felt unified.

"Good luck over there. One of our boys made this. Take it with you."

He handed John a half-dollar-sized coin. On one side was a large dog paw, and the other had Old Glory flapping in the wind. John read the back out loud.

"*Semper fi.* Always faithful." He rubbed the shiny coin as he read it. "Thanks."

They said good-bye, and he ran over to the pole where he'd last seen Emily. He scanned the crowd, but all he saw was a sea of people. The crowd was gathering around the train to see the cars that would house the devil dogs. What was getting the most attention was the car with the large, novelty, red fire hydrant. The floor was covered with hay, and the people were allowed to walk up and get a picture with the hydrant and a dog. He could see Duke was one of them. He turned away—and there she stood. Without a word, they embraced and passionately kissed. It was full of emotion. They both realized that words were not needed, and their love was real. They were both nervous, realizing this, and they simultaneously said the three magic words. They were both relieved to have said what their hearts had been saying for some time now. It was like a burning deep down, waiting to erupt. The whistle of the train broke their embrace. He held her hands, massaging them with his thumbs and slipping to a fingertip grip as they parted.

"I'll be back for you."

"I know. Keep him safe too."

She pointed to Duke. He was licking one of the kids who was rolling around in the hay. The scene made him think of Tommy.

8

LONG RIDE

"These guys have come a long way, Brass," Tomahawk proclaimed.

Brass was agreeable to a certain extent. They had come a long way, but they were all so young and green with no combat experience. They were trained up, and they could shoot straight. John was an excellent shot, as was Smiles. They all had stamina and awareness but could not be prepared for the mental and physical effects of combat.

The United States had beaten the Japanese off Guadalcanal, but there were other islands they'd migrated toward, essential points and strategic locations. The Japanese had taken Guam in December 1941. Everyone assumed that's where they would be headed. But knowledge is power, and details were kept to a minimum. "Loose lips sink ships" was as true a statement as "the sky is blue."

"I think they need some more work. Pendleton has a lot to offer," said Brass, casually referring to Camp Pendleton and their facilities.

They continued to talk in the officers' train car.

Tomahawk stared out the window, watching the scenic hills pass by. "You know. We've watched them. We've watched the dogs. I have to say they have all impressed me. Hell, they've all put on weight since getting here. They're surely eating better—the dogs and the group. The media loves them and our dogs. They're calling them devil dogs. All the newspapers and on the radio. They love them. Only in America can a dog go from the backyard to the battlefield." His Native American tone rang true inside the small train car that day.

John, Gregory, Smiles, and Ricci sat talking about things. By this time they had already made it into scenic Alabama.

"You know, on this train ride we'll see ten states. That's one fifth of the United States," Smiles said.

The train ride was thirty days, cross-country, coast to coast. Most of them had seen maybe two or three states in their lifetime, and those were seen only while traveling to Camp Lejeune. The adventure was just starting for these young marines.

O'Ryan walked into their car. "What are you queers doin' in here?" He always knew how to make an entrance and it was normally not by invitation.

"We're just talking," Smiles responded.

John interrupted, "What do you want, O'Ryan?"

"Anyone have a smoke?"

Ricci was the only one of the group who smoked, and he offered one up, probably in hopes of getting O'Ryan to leave.

O'Ryan lit the cigarette and glanced around the room, making sure to stop and make eye contact with John. He took a long pull from the cig, blew a thick cloud of smoke into the middle of the room, and left.

"Now that that asshole is gone, did you guys see the bar back there are few miles?" Ricci asked.

The train was braking to a stop.

"I saw a sign for the Stagecoach," John said.

"Hell, yes. Let's go tonight. Smiles wants to go," Ricci proclaimed.

Smiles had a big grin on his face. He was a great young man, but he was skinny, with glasses, and he would never get laid on his own. His only hope was to rely on the average-looking but confident Ricci to lead the way.

Of course, leaving the train in the middle of the night was a covert operation. They all knew Brass would kill them if they got caught. John was hesitant but eventually was talked into it. A simple question of his marine manhood was all it took. He didn't want to appear weak. They all knew he had it for Emily, but he was too good-looking to leave behind. They needed his charm and good looks to accomplish their mission. John proposed that they meet outside the dinner car and walk a few miles back to the bar.

They could hear the music as they approached the large, two-story, wooden building. The Stagecoach sign was crooked, hanging above the rickety front porch. The shady appearance gave Smiles second thoughts.

"You guys sure about this?" he questioned.

Everyone proceeded to make fun of him at that point. That lasted for a few seconds, and then they tossed their drinks into the woods and walked in. It didn't take long to find trouble. In fact, the young men may have been looking for trouble more than they were looking for women. Either way, they could find both here.

Two big cowboys took exception to the group's advances to their local bar flies. Surprisingly, Smiles was the instigator. He walked up in between the two cowboys and began talking to the girl at their table. She was receptive, but they weren't, and the biggest of the two hauled off and hit Smiles across the face with a right hook. He didn't go down, much to everyone's amazement, but the second guy picked him up and tossed him over the bar and into the wall of bottles and glasses. He gathered himself and came walking back, bloody nose and all.

John ran over to help but was hit by the big one's retracting elbow that led his fist into Smiles's face once again. He and John stood there, a bit stunned.

Ricci was sitting nearby watching—and talking to a lovely young woman.

"Aren't you going to help your friends?" she asked.

"I guess I should, huh?" he replied.

He was snatched up and thrown across the table by the second cowboy. He landed by John and Smiles. He rose to his feet, and the three stood there—wobbly, but ready for more. John jumped up and hit the biggest one in the nose, moving him off his mark a few feet. He followed it up with an uppercut that moved him back a few more feet. These cowboys were tough. They both stood there, the biggest one bleeding from his nose, and laughed.

About that time, Gregory could hear the commotion as he walked down the corridor from the washroom and back into the smoky room. He saw the effects of alcohol and exhaustion as John took another swing at one of them and missed.

"Great," he said to himself. "Here goes."

He walked over and began damage control. John, Smiles, and Ricci were arguing among themselves at this point.

"I was just supposed to be a wingman!" John yelled.

"Holy shit, my eye hurts," Smiles said.

"Holy shit is right! That thing looks bad," John replied.

"Yours doesn't look much better. Ricci! Stop smiling at her!" Smiles yelled.

Ricci was blowing kisses and mouthing words to the girl he'd been talking to before. Gregory grabbed a whiskey off the bar and took a shot.

"Okay, gentlemen, we are sorry about the mix-up. We meant no harm or disrespect. We're going to be leaving now. You have an extremely fine establishment here. Extremely well kept. God bless America," Gregory said to the two cowboys, walking backward as he left.

"You're not going anywhere, son," the biggest one said.

"Kind sir, I'm sure there has been a misunderstanding," Gregory replied.

"Like I said, you're not going anywhere," he repeated as he poked Gregory in the chest. Gregory looked over at his three buddies as they wobbled back and forth.

"Okay. Okay. I tried. So who's first? How about you, Mr. Black Teeth? Or you, Captain Fat-ass?" Gregory said, referring to their most apparent traits.

The big one grinned, revealing his horrible dental situation, and took a swing at Gregory, who ducked and countered with an uppercut that lifted the cowboy off his feet, knocked out a few of his decaying teeth, and landed him on his back, unconscious.

The other cowboy stepped in and hit Gregory on the side of his head. He then grabbed Gregory and tried to lift him up and throw him down, but Gregory weighed too much.

John hit the cowboy over the head with a bottle, knocking him out.

"Let's get the hell out of here," John said.

Gregory helped Smiles and Ricci. With each other's help, they all left the bar.

"Call me sometime," Smiles said to the girl as he was carried out.

They all stumbled back to the train, holding the cold beers they'd stolen from the bar on their eyes. They laughed at what the night had brought them. They sat outside the dogs' train car, finishing off the last of their open beers.

"These dogs have no idea what they're getting into," John said. "Shit, we don't have any idea what we are getting into. But I'm glad they are on our side."

"Me too," Gregory said. They all agreed.

"I would like to propose a toast—to our dogs. You too are marines. We will fight for you just as you will fight for us. Your noses and your eyes will keep us safe. Our guns and our knives will keep you safe. Together we cannot be defeated. Devil dogs!"

"How'd you end up here, Gregory?" John asked.

Gregory, the most sober of the bunch, explained to them that he was initially part of the marine glider program in Fort Worth. That program was eventually canceled. Besides, his size would put too much stress on a glider. John opened up about his reasons for joining the War Dog program but also about his duty to serve his country. He explained that his reason for joining the marines was an easy one: he wanted to serve his country, to keep America free. He wanted to contribute, so that when he was older he could tell his kids stories about his adventures.

"Kids? Aren't you moving a bit fast? What does Emily think of that?" slurred Smiles. They liked to give John a hard time.

"What about you, Ricci?" John asked.

"I grew up in Queens and joined on my own. I didn't really care where I ended up. I've never had a dog or any other animal before," Ricci said. He went on to describe all the rats in New York City—how they were everywhere—in the streets, in the sewers, in the walls of the buildings. He continued, "I lost my older brother in the Wall Street bombing. He was seven. It tore my parents apart. I was too young to even remember much about him. I carry his picture with me, though." He passed it around and the others sympathized with him.

"I remember my parents talking about that. Nineteen twenty, I think. I remember my mother being upset because the cowards actually blew up the horse that drew the carriage in front of the building. It killed forty people—men, women, children," John added.

"I always wanted the companionship of a big brother. You know, these dogs make me feel good, like a brother. So do you guys."

"Semper fi," John said. "Good lord, Smiles."

"What?" he replied, "My eye?"

"That too, but I think you just pissed your pants."

He just started laughing and the others joined in, careful not to get too raucous.

"I love you, Blade!" Smiles said out loud. "Let's toast them one more time."

They all carelessly yelled out, "Devil dogs," causing the dogs to wake up and bark. They all scattered back to their bunks. Gregory had to carry Smiles.

The next morning was rough. Brass woke everyone up earlier than normal. The soldiers, still feeling the effects of the night before, ran to get in line. It was hard to miss John and Smiles. Their black eyes stood out in the crowd. Thankfully, the discoloration didn't last more than a week, but Brass took notice that morning.

"Dear God. What happened to you two?" Brass questioned.

"I fell out of my bunk, sir!" Smiles replied.

"What did you fall on? A fuckin' land mine? What's your story, Private Markle?"

"I too fell from my bunk," John said.

Brass dismissed everyone to get their dogs. They were heading out in an hour. He stopped Smiles and John.

"Listen, we're all in this together, but if you two are homos then we are going to have some problems," Brass said.

They both adamantly declined the allegations. Brass knew what had happened the night before. He just liked watching them react. He used that information to gauge them as people. Typically, a bad liar was a good person, and a good liar was a bad person. That was the extent of Brass's psychological training. He read through their story. Brass noticed Gregory and Ricci looking and laughing, and he called them over to join his little party. He grabbed an old trash can close by that had been used the day before to dump leftover dinners. The stench was horrible. He placed it under their noses. They all began to gag. Smiles, with his weak stomach, proceeded to expel all the Schlitz he'd drunk the night before.

"Here's how this works. If any of you ever—I mean ever—run out like you did last night, I'll have your asses in a sling. We're about to be fighting for our lives. This shit is about to get real really quick. No more fuckin' around. For God sakes, I hope the other guys look worse than you two. Get your dogs, and get some ice on those shiners."

They all knew Lieutenant Brass was a hard-ass but they also knew he was a good man, with good intentions. They had to trust him. They had to respect him. He was the one who would lead them into battle. He would also be the one to inform their loved ones if they died.

9

TAKING A STAND

The sleeping cars were dark and quiet as the train wound around mountains and through canyons. The rhythmic sounds of the wheels constantly rotating along the steel tracks made it easy to relax at times, but at other times the train rattled and shook like it was coming apart. The night sky, which was spotted with a million twinkling stars, shone through the window into John's car as if they were there for no other reason than to provide the soldier with dim light from which to read by. He unfolded the letter from little Tommy Johnson and started reading it to himself.

> *Hi Private Markle. Please give Duke a great big hug for me. We really miss him around here. My dad says you guys are probably still training. How is Duke doing? Is he*

*the best dog there? He always finds me when
I hide from him. Mom and Dad are looking
for a new place to live, but I told them that
we need to make sure there's plenty of room for
Duke when he comes back home. I hope they
find one soon so Duke can come back and
live with us.*

*Where have you and Duke been traveling
to? I bet Duke really likes being outdoors so
much and spending times with all the other
dogs. Has he met any girl dogs he likes yet? If
he's like me, then the last thing he wants is a
girlfriend, I suppose. Please give Duke a big
hug and a good ear rub for me, and let him
know that when he gets home, it will be better
than ever.*

John laid the letter down gently on his chest and just
stared at the ceiling for a long moment. He could only
imagine how much little Tommy was missing Duke.
In fact, he started thinking about how much he was
missing Duke, since he was in his bunk and Duke was
all alone in his kennel. He had an idea. He woke the
other marines in his car and shared his master plan
with them. The plan was to sneak into the dog's sleeping quarters—cautiously, so as not to draw any un-
necessary attention from Brass—and then retrieve
their animals and quietly make their way back to their
bunks for some alone time. Then, after spending that

much-needed time with their canines, they would sneak back to the dogs' quarters and put them back in their kennels before anyone was the wiser.

It was a perfect plan, and as soon as the guys heard it they were on board.

The plan worked brilliantly, so this routine went on for a number of nights, and each night new soldiers joined in on the adventure. Before long, every soldier on the train was in on it. They would sneak off to retrieve their dogs for a few hours, take those dogs back with them to their bunks so they could spend some time with them, and then quietly put them back. It seemed the dogs missed their handlers as much as the men missed their dogs. The plan seemed to work flawlessly because nobody ever noticed what was going on. If they did they never said anything about it.

John really enjoyed having Duke next to him as he lay there comfortably on his bunk and wrote letters back to Tommy and Emily. It just made him feel more connected, and he knew that Duke was much happier being with him than locked up in his cold, isolated kennel. It seemed his brilliant idea did nothing but bring all the men even closer to their new canine best friends and strengthen the bonds that were already there.

But he really missed Emily, and with each passing day, his time away seemed to drag on and feel endless.

The train finally reached New Mexico in the early-morning hours. The mountains surrounded them like great protectors, saluting the men with their massive towering heights and snowcapped rims.

As the soldiers exited the locomotive, a large group of Spanish-speaking women showed up right on time and started handing out plates of food with lots of smiles to go along with the grub. This was an unexpected visit, but it was appreciated and very welcome.

Private Gregory smiled back at one of the women as she handed him his plate of food. He was hungry for a good old-fashioned home-cooked meal, and he also happened to love anything that resembled Mexican cuisine.

"Thank you. *Gracias*," Private Gregory said as he took his first giant bite of beans. They were spicy, just the way he liked them, and they were good—very good.

"Yes, Gracias. Mucho thank you. What is this stuff?" Private Ricci asked, not sure if he should eat it yet.

"Just eat it. Tacos and refried beans," Private Gregory replied. "You're such a pussy! Haven't you ever had Mexican food before?"

Ricci smirked and took his first bite.

"Wow. This is good. We don't eat much Mexican food where I come from."

"Shut up and eat it! This chow is good," Private Markle added. "It's got to beat military food, guys."

Smiles was the first one to stick his plate out for a refill. For a skinny bean pole of a young man, he could sure put his food away quickly, and he also loved Mexican food or anything close to it.

"Thank you," he said with a grin as his plate was filled to capacity for the second time.

"Why are they so happy to see us?" Private Markle asked, confused by their apparent adulation.

Gunnery Sergeant Tomahawk was quick to answer John's question because he'd been around these kinds of people before.

"Their husbands, brothers, and sons—the New Mexico National Guard—are stuck in the Philippines, captured by the Japs. Most here are of Mexican heritage but some are Indian. Imagine that, huh? An Indian fighting to defend America? They want their loved ones back, that's all. They see us as heroes. To them, we're the cavalry."

They all glanced up at the women in unison and could see the desperation mixed with gratitude in their eyes.

All the men ate their fill and for a few brief moments got to forget about the war that was going on.

Later that day the sun started a slow descent. The men and their dogs hurried outside to get some much-needed exercise after the big meal they all had devoured earlier. All the men and their dogs ran drills and practiced their commands. It seemed all the dogs really took to the environment right away and had no trouble at all adapting to the cold weather. After about an hour of training, the men decided to let the dogs have a little free time to roam and run.

The evening sun lit up the side of a snow-covered hill, causing it to glisten in spots as the dogs ran and hopped in and out of the snow. The handlers were trying hard to keep up with their canine friends, but that was next to impossible. The dogs were enjoying their short burst of freedom, and so were the men, but the dogs were just too fast to keep up with.

"I give up," Private Ricci said. He was exhausted. Even in the cold, beads of sweat formed over his eyebrows and dropped down into his tired eyes.

"Look at 'em go! Devil dogs!" John responded with the kind of pride a bragging father might have for his children playing a sport.

"They can use a good run. Let's just let 'em go for now. We'll signal them back in about fifteen minutes."

Duke and Blade took off as if they were racing. They ran side-by-side near the edge of the woods as they raced each other to nowhere in particular. It felt good to open up and run full throttle, and that's just what they did. Faster and faster, they raced in and out of trees and rocks as they explored every part of the mountain. The playfulness continued, until a wolf suddenly appeared out of nowhere and lunged at Blade full force, blindsiding him and sending him crashing to the ground with a thud. Blade quickly recovered, and he and Duke stood side by side, facing the wolf like the enemy he was. The wolf growled and lowered its head in attack position. The beast looked fierce with wide eyes and big shiny teeth, and it clearly wasn't there to play in the snow. After a few more tense seconds of staring, a couple more wolves appeared from the dim forest tree line and walked up to their peer and just stood there, like captors ready to devour their prey. But Duke and Blade stood their ground and showed no sign of weakness.

It was about then that Fever, Raptor, and Titan spotted what was going on from the nearby slope and hurried over to assist their friends. Now all five dogs stood shoulder to shoulder to show their strength in numbers, but the wolves were not showing any sign of backing down yet—and neither were the dogs. After a few seconds, more dogs appeared from behind the slope, and then a few more until there was a substantial pack of war dogs standing their ground against the wild animals. This was the first showdown the dogs had ever faced together, and their resolve and teamwork were impressive, even if nobody was there to witness it. The dogs snarled and growled at their enemies, not showing any sign of weakness as they stood their ground and protected their turf. Clearly, the pack of wolves were calculating their chances for success against the formidable foes, but after a few more moments of this intense standoff, the wolves finally tucked tail and ran back into the forest, intimidated and defeated by the devil dogs and their show of strength and unity. Just then the train let out a whistle, and the dogs took off running back to their handlers. They all came crashing down the snow-covered slope and boarded the train. They couldn't wait to get going.

And after a few minutes and a quick roll call, the wheels started turning and the train was moving full steam ahead once again.

10

WAR GAMES

The rest of the trip took the better part of a week, and when the train finally jolted and clanked itself to a complete stop at Camp Pendleton, the noise and movement woke up the men and their dogs who were all sharing bunks together. They had overslept and never brought their canine companions back to the dog car that night. But this particular instance was okay with Brass. He figured the more the dogs bonded with their handlers, the better for everybody. In fact, John's brilliant plan to go undetected never really worked out, but John didn't know that. He thought he and the other men were slick, but the truth was much different. Brass knew all along what was going on; he just decided there was no harm in it, so he turned a blind eye.

It was impressive the way the marines exited the train with their dogs. They marched down the steps one at a time with their well-trained dogs by their sides. It caught the attention of a short, pudgy man with a permanent scowl and a small scar over his right eye—Colonel Westinghouse, who greeted the war-dog platoons as they exited the train. Lieutenant Brass stepped off last and took a deep, cleansing breath. He was happy to not be moving anymore.

"Lieutenant Brass," Westinghouse said with authority as he introduced himself.

"Yes, sir," Brass responded as he saluted the colonel.

"Welcome to sunny California. How did the dogs fare on your trip?" the colonel asked with enthusiasm.

"Just fine, Colonel," replied Brass.

"All matters related to your dogs come to me, understand? All matters. If you need anything, let me know. I will make it happen. I am happy to see these dogs fighting alongside us. However, a few here aren't so sure about the idea of fighting with dogs," the colonel explained with a wink. He was a believer.

They continued to talk for a while. The colonel was a good man. His actions followed his words, and his reputation for being fair and impartial followed him. He wore his silver eagle insignia with pride. He'd earned it, as evidenced by the large scar above his eye. He wore the rare war eagle insignia with the eagle facing the arrows. Anyone who could tell the difference held a special place at Westinghouse's table. The wartime insignia faced the arrow, while the peacetime faced the olive branch. To know this earned respect with the colonel.

A small group of marine raiders watched the handlers as they worked with their dogs. One of the raiders just couldn't keep quiet. He yelled out as if he were talking to Lassie, imitating the famous lines from the show.

Clearly they were amusing themselves at the dog's expense. This didn't sit well with the marines. O'Ryan let Raptor go, and the dog quickly sprinted toward the raiders. He was clearly out for blood, and suddenly things got very serious as the raiders took a step back and prepared for the attack they knew was coming. Raptor rushed toward the group as they readied themselves for a fight, but at the last possible second, Private O'Ryan spared them all by yelling out to his dog.

The dog stopped short and immediately sat down in front of the raiders. They all took a deep breath as Raptor looked back at his commander for further instructions. O'Ryan called him back, and the dog quickly jogged back to his trainer like it was just another day at the office. The raiders stood there, shocked and silent. Suddenly they were at a loss for words, but they were also impressed—very impressed—and that was clear to everybody who witnessed this act of control. The other dogs sat there stoically, staring at the group of raiders and hoping they'd be called upon to attack next.

The colonel and Brass were still getting to know one another as they talked.

"Colonel, they shipped us out with limited medical supplies for our dogs," Brass explained. "Anything you could do would be greatly appreciated."

The colonel groaned a little and then smiled.

"Consider it done," Westinghouse replied.

Brass was happy to hear that. He just hoped that the colonel meant it.

"Thank you, sir."

Colonel Westinghouse continued, "Your tents are set up along the north side. Get them settled. Mess hall for dinner, eighteen hundred hours."

"Yes, sir. Thank you for everything, sir," Brass said, happy that the colonel was on board with the dogs and possibly even the much-needed supplies.

"Just be sure to keep those dogs alive. We're gonna need 'em," Westinghouse warned.

"Yes, sir!" Brass promised.

The next morning handlers found the word *Geronimo* written in several places throughout their camp. Clearly, it was a taunt from the paratroopers, exclaiming their readiness to make the jump into wartime. *Geronimo* was the term they screamed as they leapt from the planes. A few of the paratroopers watched the handlers' expressions from behind the adjacent building.

"Geronimo!" one of the paratroopers yelled out.

"Ruff! Ruff! Ruff!" the other paratrooper standing next to him joked. The two of them laughed together.

"We'll be ready next time, won't we, boys?" John was quick to ask. Brass ignored the paratroopers' childish joke. He walked over to a tent—one that wasn't there the day before. He looked inside.

"I'll be damned," Brass said as he looked at the new canine medical office set up inside the tent. It seemed the colonel had quickly made good on his promise and set up the large tent with every medical supply at his disposal. There was even a large examining table— and plenty of medicine, along with some old surgical tools. He even saw some dog treats and cow bones. He wondered how the colonel had pulled that one off.

The training area was all set up as the raiders and paratroopers participated in the day's war game. Neither the raiders nor the paratroopers had any idea what to expect from the dogs, but they were sure of one thing: they wanted to outsmart them.

John and Ricci sat in a foxhole sharing their C rations with their dogs. Nothing brings two young men closer than sitting in a foxhole together. John loved to listen to the Italian accent come from Ricci's mouth. John often tried to talk back with the accent but his long Southern drawl hindered that. It came out sounding more like a drunken Irish mobster.

Private Smiles ran up out of nowhere with some news. He adjusted his oversized glasses.

"Blade's alerting," Smiles warned.

Ricci cranked the phone to tell the others.

"The dogs are alerting. Six hundred yards, two hundred degrees. They're coming in, boys," Ricci was quick to warn.

Lieutenant Brass responded back quickly.

"Good job. Keep us updated."

Duke was alerting in the opposite direction, so Ricci cranked up the phone again.

"Sir, they're splitting up. They're moving in on both flanks."

"Send Markle and Duke out," Brass responded.

"Scout them at two hundred to the east," Ricci said, but Duke was already pointing that way.

"Let's go, boy," John ordered.

They hurried into the woods, and Duke alerted quickly. John leaned down and cranked up the phone.

"They are alongside the creek bed about two hundred yards up. They are on the move. I see 'em. The dogs are right. Give him the time and coordinates. We are going to mow these assholes down. They definitely split."

Clearly they all took the war games and training exercises seriously. The competition between them and the raiders was heated, and there was no way they'd let those clowns win, especially after that earlier display of disrespect.

"Lieutenant, we got 'em!" Ricci shouted out.

"They're gonna try to attack both flanks. When I give the order, open it up. Pin them in the creek bed," Brass ordered.

Ricci yelled for John to get back.

"I'm going in!" John yelled out.

Ricci couldn't believe what he was hearing.

"Hell, no!" Ricci responded, sure that it was a bad idea. But it was too late. Duke and John were already belly-crawling toward the creek bed.

That's when Lieutenant Brass decided it was time to light those sons of bitches up. That's also when the other flank started shooting.

"Hell, yeah!" Private Ricci yelled out in victory.

He squeezed the trigger as the blanks ejected from the massive thirty-caliber gun and fell to the ground. The ambush continued for a few more minutes because the paratroopers were dug in deep.

"Cease fire!" Brass ordered.

The gunfire came to a screeching halt. The paratroopers realized too late that they had been outmaneuvered. Fake bullets and blanks meant nothing. It was still real enough to all of them. The War Dog platoon had taken out the best of the raiders and that was something to brag about. There would be no doubt nor disrespect after that.

John and Duke sat smugly on top of the ridge, looking down on everyone else like the losers they were. That's when John, Ricci, and Private Gregory started the chant.

"Devil dogs! Devil dogs! Devil dogs!" They shouted, as the words echoed through the woods like a victory song. Everybody heard it, but there could be no
protest this time—not this time. The day went to the
devil dogs and their handlers, and everybody knew it.

The handlers, paratroopers, and raiders were all having dinner together at the Camp Pendleton mess hall.
There was lots of talk and the sound of clanking silver-
ware, along with laughs and mumbles that filled the
air. One of the paratroopers just had to break the ice
and say something about how the day went.

"You guys did pretty good out there today. Those
dogs are something else," he said as he nodded and
grinned.

"Hell yes, they are!" one of the raiders added.

"I'd never have thought it possible until I saw it
with my own eyes," the trooper added with his mouth
half-full. Brass showed up to add in his two cents.

"They're naturally trusting animals so you have to
always think about how they are going to react to what
you're asking them to do. They are always faithful, always," Brass explained.

Suddenly all the handlers started their "devil dog"
chant again. The paratroopers and raiders joined, in
solidifying their belief in the handlers and their canine marines.

Clearly they had won them over. They had show-cased their dogs' talents, and coupled with their own training, had proven their worth. And most important-ly, they all welcomed anything that could potentially save their lives on the battlefield and give them the slightest edge. It appeared that the devil dogs could achieve both.

"Calm down, men. We'll have the camp to ourselves soon. The troopers and raiders are shipping out in the morning," Brass explained. John smiled; he loved that everybody seemed to be getting along so well.

"Last night here, huh? Too bad..." John said, a little sad that they couldn't spend more time getting to know each other, now that the dogs had earned their respect as soldiers. One of the raiders pulled out a camera and requested that all of the men and their dogs line up for a picture. They all protested a little, but finally they all lined up with John and Duke right in the center to have their picture taken. The Raider clicked a few pic-tures off and then grinned.

"Gotta have a record of these here devil dogs, so when they're famous, I can say I helped shape them into the amazing soldiers they will be." Everybody laughed.

The next morning brought with it lots of surprises. The raiders and troopers woke up and quickly jumped out of their beds, ready to face the new day. Instead, they jumped right into multiple piles of dog crap stra-tegically placed by their bedsides.

"What the hell!" one of the paratroopers mumbled in disgust as he held his nose and tried to wipe off his foot.

"Son of a bitch!" another raider yelled out.

They hurried outside and ran right into a line of handlers with their dogs sitting on point. Brass grinned as he saw how much discomfort the men were in.

"It's just our way of saying good-bye and good luck over there, men!" Brass explained. That's when Gunnery Sergeant Tomahawk had to weigh in as well.

"Soldiers. Keep your heads down. Not only will it save you from getting them shot off, it will also keep you from stepping in dog shit," he explained.

They all started shaking hands and laughing.

"Get your shit together, men! No pun intended. It's time to get moving," the paratroopers' sergeant ordered. As the paratroopers hugged the handlers to say their good-byes, they secretly tried to wipe off their feet on the handler's pants, but the subtle revenge didn't work.

The groups boarded their boats and prepared to head to the Pacific. The handlers were happy to see them go. It left them to themselves over most of the camp.

Lieutenant Brass walked into the mess hall and couldn't believe his eyes. He saw tons of food that the others had left behind.

The men decided to chow down on all the great leftovers as the dogs sat outside eating prime rib. Ricci decided it was a good time to lighten things up with a few jokes. The problem was that most of the time his jokes weren't that funny. But maybe he had some new ones to share.

"So, a Jap man walks into the currency exchange in New York City with two thousand yen and walks out with seventy-two dollars. The following week, he walks in with another two thousand yen and walks out with sixty-six dollars. He asks the teller why he got less money that week than the one before. The teller said, 'Fluctuations.' The Jap storms out, and just before slamming the door, he turns around and shouts, 'Fuck you, Americans!'"

Everyone laughed except for Smiles.

"Fluctuations. Fuck you Asians," John repeated.

Not to be outdone, Smiles decided he had one too. The problem was, Smiles was even worse at telling jokes.

"I got one. Okay, here goes. An American man was sitting in his favorite restaurant when a Jap said to him, 'I am sick of seeing your big, round eyes.' The American replied, 'Put on a blindfold, then.' The Japanese man asked, 'Where do I get one?' The American then said, 'Here, take my shoelace.'"

Everyone just sat there for a moment before yelling out loud boos and shaking their heads—it was awful.

"Gregory, you know any jokes?" Ricci asked. "Somebody must have some good jokes to tell."

"I'm not much of a joke teller," replied Private Gregory. That didn't come as a surprise to any of them.

The stature and stern features that Gregory wore like a badge of honor made him seem like a rock wall with little room for laughter or feelings.

"What?" John questioned. "You got to know a joke or two? It's got to be better than Smiles."

Gregory decided to give it a try. "Okay, here's one my father told me. What do you call a Jap that has only one ball?"

Everyone went silent.

"Whatwentwong. Get it? Whatwentwong!" Gregory explained. After a few seconds, everybody started laughing, spitting out their drinks and choking on their fine meal. It was the best joke of the day. Who would have thought?

The sun peaked over the horizon on February 14, 1944, casting a magical orange stream of light across the rippling Pacific Ocean. The soldiers stood around staring at the old ship that was supposed to transport them across the Pacific. It looked more suited for a junkyard.

"That piece of shit is gonna get us across the ocean?" Private Cammacho asked with disdain in his tone.

"Let's hope so," John responded.

Cammacho took another discouraging look.

"Look at it! The son of a bitch is about to sink. There's no way that thing is going to make it. We're going to be on that for two months? I'd rather swim."

Brass stepped forward to try and reassure them that the vessel was seaworthy, even though he wasn't really sure of that himself yet.

"That can be arranged. Quiet down, Cammacho. It will straighten out once it takes on some fuel and cargo." At least that's what Brass hoped would happen.

Parts of the hull looked warped and appeared wavy in places. The deck seemed flimsy at best. The side rails were clearly missing parts and the lopsided way it sat in the water gave nobody reason to believe that this vessel could ever make it out of port. It was also rusty, ugly, and looked more suited for scrap metal than anything else. Everyone hoped there were plenty of life jackets on board.

11

OUT TO SEA

On the ship deck, the handlers and their dogs jogged in circles, running past the dog crates that were all lined up and facing seaward. They worked on commands and discipline.

"You dogs got the best view around," John joked.

"It sure beats ours. I thought I was going to sweat to death last night. We're right above the engine room," Private Gregory complained.

They leaned against the shaky rail and enjoyed the ocean view.

Private Smiles weighed in on the conversation. "At least no one is shooting at us," he pointed out.

"Not yet!" John added. "That will happen later."

Lieutenant Bittick appeared and stood in front of them like a statue awaiting reanimation. "Listen up!" Bittick yelled.

The men ran and formed a line.

"Welcome aboard, men. We've got two months together, most of it on this boat. We have established some guidelines. One, every morning you will conduct exercises and jog with your dogs. You will then crate them and proceed to chow. After breakfast everyone will participate in cleaning the vessel. This means everyone. The dogs use the poop deck located at the rear of the ship. We will not leave any type of trail for the enemy to follow. The farther we get, the more hostile the waters are. Lunch is served at thirteen hundred hours. After lunch you will clean yourself and your weapons. At sixteen hundred hours, we will gather on deck for more exercises and then feed the dogs. Dinner is at eighteen hundred hours. Everyone got that?"

All the handlers yelled, "Yes, sir!"

Darkness on the sea had its own brand of beauty as the handlers worked with their dogs on the ship's deck. The moonlight shimmered and glistened off the gentle ocean waves that seemed to have an almost musical rhythm to them that night. The salt air and gentle breeze seemed to be the final touch on an almost picture-perfect night at sea. But things were about to change.

That night they were training their dogs to locate a stuffed Japanese uniform that resembled a Japanese soldier. Duke was hot on the trail as he roamed and sniffed around with great vigor.

"That's it, Duke. Good boy!" John said as he petted Duke and reassured him he was doing well.

"Get 'em, Raptor. Find 'em, boy," Private Gregory urged, wanting his dog to be the first to find the decoy.

The dogs all sniffed around until finally Fever found the dummy and alerted.

"Hell, yeah! Heel!" Gregory ordered, happy to be the first one to locate the dummy.

Fever grabbed the decoy with his teeth and pulled the dummy out from under the boxes. That's when Duke decided he'd had enough. He ran over and tried to take the dummy away from Fever by force. They growled at each other for a second, and each stood his ground as if a fight were about to ensue, but both dogs were just trying to show themselves as strong. Fever stood there and faced Duke with a false bravado that had everybody fooled except for Duke. After a few more seconds of intense snarling and growling, Fever finally backed down. After all, he knew he was no match for Duke, and so did John.

"Good boy, Duke," John said as he tried hard not to grin. That's when Duke did something nobody expected. He raised his left leg and pissed all over the Japanese dummy. John couldn't hold it in any longer; he laughed hard.

"I believe we have a winner!" Private Ricci exclaimed.

Later that night, out on the ship's deck, John wrote a letter to Emily and Tommy. He missed Emily and wondered what she was doing that very second. It seemed that his letter writing had become his secret way of pretending she was there with him. And little Tommy—well, John felt a special connection with the boy because of Duke. He knelt down beside Duke's crate as the winds picked up and whistled through the old vessel. The night was still beautiful, but it felt like there might be a storm brewing.

"Hey boy. You staying cool out here? You see any land yet? Look at that moon. This must be the most peaceful place around, huh? No wars, no fighting, no governments. Just empty space, water, and lots of sky. We should move here when this is all over. Just me, you, and Emily. That would be real nice."

The night sky filled with a few dark clouds. The breeze picked up slightly, and the gentle waves smacked up against the hull of the ship. Rapid gunfire rang out and sent hot lead streaking into the dark ocean and broke the apparent calm of the evening. John rushed back to the stern to find several of the soldiers standing around with crazy-eyed Lieutenant Bittick right in the middle.

"You see it?" Bittick asked.

"No," responded Brass.

They were firing at a dim red light off the back of the boat several hundred yards away.

"Dammit! Get off the gun!" Bittick ordered. Then he slid behind the weapon and opened fire, smiling the entire time. He ceased fire after putting hundreds of shell casing on the deck.

"I don't see it," Brass admitted.

Gunnery Sergeant Tomahawk responded quickly, "Me either. You think it went back down? That's never a good thing!"

The wind picked up and the waves began to crash over the bow of the boat as the men peered out into the night sky and open waters.

"I think Bittick is a senile old man. Besides, we have something else to worry about," Brass pointed out toward the rippling waves. The peaceful night at sea they had enjoyed earlier was quickly turning into rough waters.

The ocean began to rage all around them almost instantly. The waves crashed hard into the vessel's side, sending the soldiers flying all over the deck as they scrambled to get below. The big old ship struggled not to broach as the calm suddenly turned violent and the storm worsened by the second. Those dark clouds that had formed earlier had friends, and those friends kicked up violent waves and fierce winds. Monster waves jutted up from the sea. They formed huge curls and smashed into the side of the ship with apparent motive. Clearly, the love story between the ocean and the ship was over, and what was left seemed like a jilted lover as the ocean pitched the large ship around as if it were a child's toy.

And it was no different for the men below. They too were being tossed around like rag dolls.

"I can't take much more of this," Private Smiles moaned as he covered his mouth, trying hard not to lose his chicken fried steak all over the floor.

"You better take that shit outside, Smiles. Don't you dare puke on us," Ricci ordered. But Smiles couldn't hold it down one more second, and with a violent heave, he threw up everywhere—and on Ricci. The men groaned in disgust as they fled his immediate vicinity as if he were on fire. Ricci just stood there, and it looked like he'd be the next one to toss his cookies.

The boat was being thrown around like a small toy boat in a bathtub. The whitecaps continued to smash into the side like battering rams. Meanwhile, up on deck, Bittick continued to fire hundreds of rounds as Brass ran toward the steps and then down to the sleeping quarters.

"Get your dogs, and get down below! Now! Move it! Move it!" Brass ordered.

He made it belowdecks and continued to bark out orders.

"Get your dogs off the deck, and get below now! Move it! Dear God, son! What the hell is going on down here! Can't you pansies stand a few small waves?" Brass yelled with a sly grin.

Just then a huge rogue wave crashed into the side of the boat, throwing everyone to the floor.

Up on the bridge, Captain Stone, a bulky old man in his sixties, struggled to control the ship in the rough seas, but it seemed near impossible.

"Hold it, hold it!" he ordered.

The boat was suddenly thrust in the opposite direction, preventing it from tilting all the way over to one side.

Captain Stone cursed the ocean, bringing meaning to the old phrase "cussing like a sailor."

"Is she going to hold up, Captain?" Tomahawk asked in a panicked voice. And even as the words were escaping his lips, he knew he shouldn't have said it.

Captain Stone just stared at him intently. He couldn't believe the man had the guts to ask him that.

"I'll throw your ass overboard if you ever ask me that again! We've been through worse storms than this little sprinkle! You doubt me?"

Tomahawk acknowledged with a slight nod that he did not doubt the captain. He knew better than to say too much. In fact, he quickly decided it might be a good time to leave the good captain to his business before he did indeed get thrown overboard.

"I'm going to help belowdecks!" Tomahawk said as he hightailed it off the bridge.

Up on the deck, the handlers struggled to remove their dogs from the crates. Thunder boomed and lightning strikes rattled the air as the sea grabbed one of the crates with a dog still in it and pulled it overboard.

Private Davis screamed out as he noticed what was happening. He ran to the edge and nearly jumped overboard trying to save his dog. He was quickly grabbed by John at the last possible second, but the crate and dog were gone, apparently swallowed up by the sea. Davis stood there and searched the rough seas for any sign of the crate, but all he could see were white caps and big waves.

"Get down below! Now! He's gone! He's gone!" John yelled out. But Davis just stood there, so John grabbed him by the arm and pulled him away. They all finally made it below. John struggled to keep Davis below; he just couldn't stand the thought of leaving his dog behind. It took a little while, but Davis finally realized there was nothing he could do.

Down in the sleeping quarters, they were all crammed together tightly into the small space with their dogs close by. After another hour of strong seas, the storm finally eased up, and Smiles started mopping up the mess he'd made earlier.

"Who was shooting the Mark Two?" Private O'Ryan asked. Nobody said a word. The Mark Two was a fifty-millimeter gun retrofitted to several merchant ships utilized as wartime vessels. It was a powerful weapon with the potential to do much damage to its target.

"Bittick. There was a Jap sub," John explained.

"Did he hit it?" O'Ryan asked.

"It disappeared as soon as the storm kicked up," explained John.

"You think they're tracking us?" Gregory was quick to ask.

Brass emerged from the doorway.

"All right, men. Looks like we survived the storm. Is everyone accounted for?" he asked as he looked around, counting heads.

"Sir, we lost one. The water grabbed the crate and took him overboard," Ricci responded.

"Whose was it?" Brass asked.

"Sir, I believe it was Davis's dog, Shiner," Ricci explained.

"Dammit. Davis?" He was not happy to hear that.

Brass looked around and spotted Davis sitting in the far corner with his head in his hands. He walked over to him and put his hand on Davis's shoulder in a comforting way.

"Sir!" Davis moaned.

"Stop crying, Davis. It was a freak accident. It could have been any one of these dogs," Brass explained. "You need to deal with it, and by that, I mean join the rest of us."

Davis nodded an agreement.

The night was filled with grief for the lost animal, but the handlers would keep their dogs even closer than they had before because they realized Brass was right; it could have been any of the dogs that went overboard that night.

The next morning Captain Stone ran down into the sleeping quarters like he'd just won the lottery.

"Wake up! Wake up!" he commanded

"What is it, Captain?" Gregory asked, still half-asleep.

"Get to the deck! Hurry!" Stone ordered.

"Oh God, I hope it's land," John muttered.

"We can only hope, I think," Ricci said as he rubbed his tired eyes.

They all piled up top with their dogs by their sides. Brass rounded the corner and saw everybody.

"What are you doing up here?" Brass asked, shocked to see them all standing there so early.

"Sir, Captain Stone woke us," Gregory answered.

"Look! Look!" Stone pointed out.

They all leaned over the rail and gasped in disbelief.

"Oh my God!" John said with a big smile.

"Shiner! Shiner!" Davis yelled out when he saw the crate and Shiner resting in one of the cargo nets hung from the side of the vessel.

"Holy shit, Shiner! You son of a bitch! Oh my God!" Davis yelled out.

"I'll be damned. Get his ass up here!" Brass ordered.

They lifted the crate to the edge of the bow and pulled Shiner aboard.

"Get me a sheet! Now! Get me a sheet!" Brass ordered.

A handler hurried up to Brass with a sheet. They laid it on the ground and were about to place Shiner on it, but he let out a weak moan. Maybe all wasn't well after all.

"Careful now. He's in bad shape," Brass pointed out.

"Come on, buddy. I need you. Come on now," Davis pleaded.

The dog was taken down to the ship's sick bay. Brass and Davis were huddled around Shiner as they worked on the dog. Brass palpated the animal like a vet would do and used his skills to revive the dog. Clearly Brass had done this before, and the way he gently handled the dog as he worked on him was impressive and endearing.

"He's definitely lame in this leg. My fear is internal injury. He had to have been thrown around pretty bad. I can't believe he lived. I'm going to keep him here," Brass announced.

He gave Shiner an injection.

"Get some sleep, Shiner," Brass added.

"Thanks, Lieutenant," Davis said. "I think you missed your calling. You'd make a great vet!"

Suddenly, a loud bell sounded out.

"Land ho, Private Davis," Brass announced.

Up on the ship's deck, Stone yelled, "Land ho!"

"You think there are any hookers on this island?" Ricci questioned as he grinned and licked his chops.

"I'm sure the First Division already ran through them like water through a pipe," Gregory replied.

"At this point, I'll take some sloppy seconds," Ricci was quick to point out.

"I don't think you'll be just the second," John smirked.

12

LUNGA POINT

Smaller transport boats pulled alongside their vessel, and the marines began to pile in.

The small boat's captain was quick to welcome them all. "Welcome to Lunga Point, marines. Guadalcanal, April 10, 1944, and free from the Japs!" he said with a big smile.

They were happy to make land after being at sea for nearly sixty days. It would take a while for them to regain their land legs. Everyone piled into the small boats. The men finally reached the Lunga Point Beach in the dead of night, so the marines ended up putting their gear up under a bright full moon.

"Damn, I'm hungry," Smiles announced as he rubbed his stomach.

"I wonder if anyone is going to feed us," added Ricci.

"Break out the rations. I'm going to feed Blaze," Smiles said with an urgent tone.

"Duke—you hungry, boy? Can you believe we're about to go to war? The real shit, not some demo drills or games. Real bullets. Real bombs. Real death!" John wasn't sure he was ready for all that, but he knew he needed to be. He hated the idea of war—and especially the taking of another life—but he reconciled in his own mind that if it came down to "kill or be killed," he could kill. After all, that's what the training was all about. Tucked away back in his mind, John still wondered if, when the time came and he was forced to look his enemy in the eyes before shooting, he'd be able to pull the trigger.

"Crazy to think they've given us the right to kill people. You ever killed anyone?" Ricci asked John.

"I've never been put in that situation. I had to put a horse down before. He broke his two front legs jumping a creek. Got one caught in a crevice. Almost snapped it right off. The other leg broke when he fell down the creek bed."

"Damn. So how did you do it?" Gregory asked.

"Gregory, pass me a Schlitz. My father handed me the gun. I was eleven. I never so much as shot a possum before that day. He told me that there was no way to fix his legs. He was suffering. If we didn't do it, the coyotes would eat him alive."

"I've never seen a coyote before," Ricci admitted.

"Where did you get these cigars, Smiles?"

"Off the supply ship."

"That was you? They've been trying to figure out who stole all that shit," Gregory explained.

"All I took was a couple boxes of cigars," admitted Smiles as he blew some smoke rings into the night air.

"And some liquor," he added. He pulled out a bottle.

"I'll be damned. Smiles has a wild side to him after all," Ricci joked.

"I'm a crazy man!" Smiles admitted as he took a big drink. "Continue, Markle,"

"So, my father handed me the Winchester. One shot put him out of his misery. My dad had brought him home the day I was born. We named him Duke. He was just a small colt. It was one of the toughest days of my life."

"No shit," Ricci said.

"It's fate that Duke is my dog," explained John.

They all went silent for a moment, reflecting on the story.

"I got to piss," announced John.

"Me too," added Gregory.

They walked over to a line of palm trees and began to relieve themselves side by side.

"That's some heavy shit, Markle," Gregory admitted.

"You believed that?" John asked with a smile.

"What do you mean? You just lied to everyone?" Gregory wasn't sure now what was true and what wasn't. He always took John as a straight shooter.

"Not really. I mean I shot the horse," admitted John.

"His name wasn't Duke, was it?" Gregory asked.

"I don't even remember his name," John admitted.

"What? Markle, look at those men over there," Gregory said as he glanced in their direction. The men were nestled up on their dogs.

"I mean, come on," Gregory pleaded.

"Look at 'em," John grunted. "They're over there jawin' about what they would do in that situation. Would they do it? Could they do it to their dog if the circumstances called for it? Their minds are working. Mental preparation is eighty percent of surviving," explained John.

"Tell me about it. I think a mosquito just bit my dick. Damn, these bugs are horrible. Was it even a horse you shot?" Gregory asked as he grinned.

"Maybe," replied John.

They turned to walk back to the others.

"I guess it was more of an old-ass donkey. He actually fell off the side of the loading trailer," admitted John.

They both laughed as they made their way back to the group.

The next morning, the soldiers were stuck in their tents as the sheets of rain came crashing down in Coconut Grove. All the men immediately jumped up at attention as General Pelt walked up.

"Good afternoon, men. Welcome to Coconut Grove, the finest place on the island. We have heard a lot about these dogs, and while I believe there is some merit to what I've heard, some are not so quick to entrust their lives to our four-legged friends. We will begin field exercises in two days. These exercises will help you survive on your mission. It's miserable here—and even more miserable out there. It rains like a son of a bitch. The bugs are a motherfucker. And you have people trying to kill you. But that will not cause you to fail. Only you can cause you to fail. You will succeed," General Pelt said with great passion in his voice.

Everyone yelled out, "Yes, sir!"

"That's the spirit men. That's the spirit. Brass, come see me," Pelt ordered.

He and Brass began walking in the rain together.

"Brass, we're aware of the good things a few of those dogs contributed to while in Bougainville. They did a damn good job. Personally, I'm happy to have them on our side," Pelt said.

"Thank you, sir. We actually have one of those dogs with us now. Fever. He's a mean son of a bitch, sir. Extremely loyal."

"That's good. That's good to hear. This campaign is going to be tough. Your group is being assigned to the twenty-first. I will be calling a meeting of all COs and officers in the next few days with more details. Brass, we are about to take this war to the Japs. We took this island from them, and dammit, we can do it again. This is going to be the turning point in this war. Your dogs are going to help us do this," Pelt announced.

"Thank you, sir." Brass was happy for the general's enthusiasm.

The handlers and their dogs walked through the Guadalcanal jungle, talking and simulating scout maneuvers, when they saw the natives gathering by the jungle's edge close to the beach.

"Over there. Let's go," Lieutenant Brass said.

"Request permission to visit the locals," John asked.

"Go ahead. Take Smiles and Gregory with you," Brass ordered.

"Sir, I request permission as well," O'Ryan yelled out.

"Go ahead. We will circle back in twenty," explained Brass.

They proceeded over to meet the locals. There were two Chamorro men, three women, one of whom was pregnant, and two small children. The soldiers split up as they walked through the group. The natives were clearly afraid of the dogs' presence in their area. The women quickly grabbed the children and pulled them away as if to protect them from wild beasts.

"Oh no. No, it's okay. Friendly," John explained.

They didn't seem to understand him, so he tried his tongue at the Chamorro expression for *friend*. He had picked up a bit their language from some of the other soldiers a few nights before, nothing more than a few words.

"*Hafa ga'chong,*" John said, hoping he got it right.

The women smiled, which told him he did.

"Hafa ga'chong."

"Hafa ga'chong?" one of the Chamorro women asked with a confused look on her face. She pointed to Duke when she said it.

"Yes, yes, Duke. His name is Duke. Hafa ga'chong," John said again as he petted Duke showing him to be the gentle pet that he was.

"Here. You want to pet him?" John asked the woman. She was reluctant at first but smiled.

"Here, watch this," John added.

The children wandered over with the men.

"You ready, Duke?"

John gave the handle signal to roll over. The children giggled and smiled as they watched the fierce dog act like a puppy. Then more children showed up out of nowhere as Duke delighted everybody with his playfulness.

"Oh, you like that. You like that? Watch this," John bragged.

He gave the signal to lie and crawl. Duke crawled about five feet on his belly and then just stopped. The children jumped up and down and cheered the feat, but a small girl was clearly not convinced yet that Duke was not going to devour her whole. John noticed her demeanor, so he gently took the little girl's hand and rubbed it on Duke. That's when another child, one of the men, and one of the women walked over to Smiles and Gregory and stared at their dogs.

"Hafa ga'chong," the little Chamorro girl said enthusiastically.

John looked back to see the other Chamorro people smiling and laughing. He also saw O'Ryan sitting on the beach alone, with only his dog to keep him company. He made eye contact with Gregory and nodded in the direction of O'Ryan.

Gregory acknowledged the gesture.

"Hafa ga'chong. Hafa ga'chong," John repeated.

John and Duke got up and made their way to O'Ryan. They arrived to see him weeping silently. Gregory and Titan followed behind.

"What's the problem?" Gregory asked.

"You all right?" asked John. O'Ryan shook his head.

"It's tough out here," John acknowledged.

"Out here? We're on friendly soil now. Holy shit! Oh my God! This isn't happening. Man, no it's not!" O'Ryan screamed, clearly out of control and suddenly faced with his own mortality. O'Ryan was as tough as they came, but it seemed that lately his more sensitive side was taking over. Perhaps it was the thought of dying, or maybe he just wasn't ready to admit to himself that his hard exterior hid more than just his internal organs; it hid all his insecurities too.

"Pull it together, O'Ryan," Gregory ordered.

"Look at them!" O'Ryan pointed back at the Chamorro. "Look at them! What the fuck? Why? The Japs just killed them! For what? And we're going to go kill them—and for what? So someone can say they own this fucking island? Oh God! They're going to make murderers out of all of us!" He was defeated in his mind.

The Chamorro lived peacefully on the island until the Japanese attacked in 1941. The Imperial Japanese Army called the island *Omiya Jima*, or "the great shine island." The natives were friends of the United States and often hid soldiers in their camps. The Japanese searched their camps, executed any soldiers they discovered, and would slaughter all the natives in the village, often leaving their mangled remains in plain sight as a warning to others who aided their enemy.

"Pull it together!" John, repeated.

John grabbed O'Ryan and pulled him up.

"Pull it together, O'Ryan. Now!"

"Come on. Keep it together. We got a lot more to go through. It's too early in this to lose it," Gregory explained.

O'Ryan fell back into the sand, and the rest of them followed suit. The Chamorro walked over and stood in silence.

"Hafa ga'chong," the Chamorro woman said.

"Hafa ga'chong," the little Chamorro girl repeated.

Duke licked her face. She started to giggle, eventually causing O'Ryan to follow. Everyone joined in as the tension faded.

The next day, the handlers and their dogs jogged down the main roadway past the other marine units. The other marines poured out from their tents to catch a glimpse. All the handlers were chanting as their boots hit the ground.

"Boom boom chugalug a boom boom chugalug a boom boom chugalug a boom boom. Devil dogs! Boom boom chugalug a boom boom chugalug a boom boom chugalug a boom boom. Devil dogs!"

"Who are we?" Brass shouted out.

All the handlers responded, "Devil dogs!"

They stopped in unison and ran through all the hand signals with their dogs.

Some of the other marines were clapping for them as they continued their march down the road.

Later that night the handlers were having a quiet night with their peers and dogs. Duke nipped at the bugs as John continued to write a letter. He pulled out the locket that Emily had given him. He started to reflect.

"Hey, boy, how in the world did we get here? I know how you got here, but how in the hell did *I* get here? I mean war. Why is there war? Why has the world chosen to fight each other instead of coming together? It's messed up, Duke. You don't even know, and that's a blessing for you, boy. God made you for your unconditional love. To teach us humans what real love is. Humans, we'll never learn to love like you."

John put his head in his hands and shook his head. "Never. What do we do? We take the only animal that loves unconditionally and train it to attack. We've taken what God gave you and fucked it up. I wonder what he thinks about that?"

"I think he wants us to stay alive, and these dogs are going to help us," Brass suggested.

"Sir, I didn't see you there," John jumped up, startled.

"John, I love these animals as much as you do. I don't want to lose any of them. What's in your hand there?" Brass asked.

"It's a locket," John replied.

"From that young lady back at Lejeune?" Brass grinned as he said it.

"How'd you know?"

Brass asked him to take a seat. Brass took a seat next to him, rubbing Duke's head.

"I ain't blind. She's a keeper. I've watched her work these dogs. She cares for them, no doubt about that. She must really like you. You like her?" Brass asked in a more serious tone.

"Yes, sir. I do. We love each other. I think I have some competition, though," John replied.

"Who might that be?" Brass was curious.

"O'Ryan," John explained.

Brass laughed a little.

"O'Ryan? What makes you think that?" Brass asked.

"He tried to start some shit with me at Lejeune. He was talking about how I need to stay away from her," explained John.

Brass laughed a bit more.

"Markle, you silly son of a bitch. O'Ryan is her cousin!"

"How do you know this?" John was quick to ask.

"I know everything. That's why I'm a lieutenant."

"I'll be damned," John replied as he scratched his head.

"She wants you to fight for it," Brass explained.

"For what?"

"Good Lord, son. Her love! She wants you to fight for her love. It's not going to come easy. Nothing in life will come easy. You're one of the smart ones. Figure it out. I gotta run. You two have a good night. Get some sleep. We got a long day tomorrow."

John took another look at the locket.

It was time to leave Guadalcanal and head to Guam. The soldiers boarded a boat overnight and prepared themselves for what was ahead of them. They needed to be mentally ready and know what to expect.

General Pelt addressed the group of young marines on the deck of the ship. In a loud voice he announced, "Marines, good day yesterday. It was the last day for maneuvers. It is crucial that every last one of you know your place and know it well. Your lack of knowing will result in your fellow marine's death. Look around, soldiers. Take a good look at the people next to you," General Pelt suggested.

The marines looked around.

"Chances are, either the person to your left or the person to your right won't make it back. Many of these men have families, friends, and loved ones. They want them to return safe. You must know your surroundings at all times in order for that to happen. In two days we will begin our move in the repatriation of Guam and bring liberty back to the island, to our country, to our land. How are we going to do this? We are going to kill the Japs!" Pelt said with passion in his voice.

The night air was hot and humid aboard the ship. The men were gathered up belowdecks, sweating in the heat. The sound and vibrations of constant bombing filled the ship's bowels. The occasional spray of machine-gun fire from the passing planes rattled the ship.

Many had nervous looks on their face. The men emerged up on deck to a glorious display of tracers, mortar shells, and explosions ravishing the island. Fifty-foot flames burned up the lush foliage.

"Shit. You think they would all be dead by now," Gregory pointed out.

"We could only be so lucky," Smiles added.

John rubbed his locket.

"You all right, Markle?" Smiles asked.

"I'm fine. I'm just ready to get it going. Live or die, I'm just ready," John explained with new vigor.

Private Cammacho put up a salute and began to sing "The Star Spangled Banner." After a few seconds, John joined in with him.

It didn't take long before all the handlers were on deck with their dogs and joining in on the proud moment. Private Smiles gathered his bugle and started adding some instrumental to the singing.

The marines were all proudly singing aloud arm in arm as they watched the awesome display of American military force light up the island and the night sky. It was an amazing moment as the men embraced the song as their own.

The next day Brass and Tomahawk sat in their quarters discussing the coming days. "The others will be landing on Red Beach and Blue Beach. We'll be moving on Green Beach. We will push forward about ten miles, and hopefully, if it goes as planned, we will hook up with the First Provisional Brigade. It's going to be hell, those ten miles," Brass explained.

"Sir, they're shelling the daylights out of that island. We're going to run into pockets of resistance, embedded Japs hanging on to their last hope for survival. What scares the shit out of me is when that hope is gone. They'll stop at nothing," Tomahawk pointed out.

"Let's go talk to these men," Brass said.

"Marines, today is the first day of the rest of your lives. You have all become men. Today you will have the opportunity to show it. To let your country and your fellow countrymen know that we are strong, that we fight for what is right, that we are the first to stomp on evil and crush it into the dirt. We are the marines! It's not going to be easy. You know what needs to be done. The Japs know what needs to be done. But we are going to do it better. We are going to do it harder, and we will do it longer! We are the marines!" Brass yelled out with conviction.

The men started cheering the speech.

"All right, quiet down. The Southern Task Force has been blowing the hell out of that island for days. Don't get complacent out there. They are embedded, deeply embedded, and we will use our skills, our dogs' skills, our muscle, and our brains to find them and liberate this great American territory. The inhabitants of this island depend on you. We have more firepower, we are better trained, and we are fighting for freedom. Men, my fellow marines, it has been a pleasure serving with you. I say that now because I want each and every one of you to know it. If you need anything, Tomahawk and myself are here for you. Godspeed, marines." Brass said.

The loudspeaker crackled and suddenly burst to life.

"Stand by to enter boats," Pelt commanded.

There were mixed emotions in the group. Smiles began to throw up nervously. Gregory and Cammacho smacked each other, looking for a rush of adrenaline. The dogs sat stoically as if nothing were happening. John shook a few hands and headed over to the corner. He started reading the last letter from Emily.

> *Private John Markle, I hope this letter finds you well. I know it is close to time for you to enter battle. I want you to be safe. I need you to be safe. You have to return to me, John. My soul longs for you. I am having these dreams—dreams about us and our future. We're sitting on our front porch watching the little ones playing in the yard with Duke. We are all so happy. We have our little house with the picket fence, and the neighbors all wave as they drive by. Oh John, please tell me this is not a dream. Please come back safe to me. I need to feel you in my arms. I need to be in your arms. Come back to me, John. Come back to me.*

The loud speaker started to crack, interrupting his reading.

"All men to the deck! Man your boats! Man your boats!" Pelt ordered.

"Let's take this war to 'em, boy!" John said with vigor.

He led Duke to the side of the vessel, strapped him in, and started to lower him down into the transport boat with the rest of the dogs.

"Let's go! Let's go! Keep your helmets on at all times. When you're sleeping, shitting, pissing, shooting, eating, screwing. You do not take it off! Let's go! Let's go! Go! When you hit the beach, you run and don't stop! Make it to the tree line and dig in! Let's go men, let's go!" Brass ordered.

13

GUAM

On the morning of July 20, 1944, the transport ships took the soldiers to the edge of Green Beach in Guam. The battleships were bombarding the upper ridge. Inside one boat sat John, Smiles, O'Ryan, Gregory, and their dogs. Various other soldiers filled the boat as well. John looked around as the noise of the battle faded from his ears. He saw one soldier vomiting, another rubbing a cross, one praying. Another soldier was gritting his teeth in anger. The waves were crashing against the sides of the boats. He stared up at the sun and flashed back to his childhood. He had quick visions of his mother, of playing as a child, of his life on the farm—and then his father appeared. He envisioned them talking while he taught John how to shoot a rifle.

"See, son, hold it right here," Roy said as he stood behind him and gently held the firearm in place.

"Like this?" young John replied, trying hard to get it right and please his father.

"Just like that. Now put this right up against your shoulder and look right down those sights and line it up," Roy added. He was proud of his son as he watched the young boy struggle to keep the rifle steady.

He peered down the rifle and squeezed the trigger, and with a loud bang, he fell backward with the help of the blast.

"Oh boy. You okay?" Roy asked him, helping him up.

They both laughed. Roy looked around and saw the can knocked off the fence post.

"Not bad, Tommy." Roy was proud of his boy.

"I got it," John said.

"You got it. You sure did!" Roy repeated.

John's vision faded back into the bright light of the sun. He took one more look around and witnessed hundreds of landing crafts hitting the shores as well as heavy tanks smashing into the water all around them and pulling up onshore.

"We got boots on the ground!" Brass said with authority.

Other marines ran across the beach, trying to keep themselves moving, which made them harder to hit. The marines scattered as the explosions hit, throwing several of the men into the air and dismembering them instantly. The US tanks provided heavy cover fire to the top of the ridge, but it wasn't always enough.

One pillbox continued to mow down marines as they climbed the hill. The large machine gun protruded from the small slit in the concrete box that was embedded in the side of the hill. It was well protected and hard to target.

"Get ready, marines! Keep that helmet on! Run like hell until you cross the beach road and hunker down in the hillside! You got that, Tomahawk?" Brass exclaimed.

"Yes, sir!" Tomahawk yelled.

The dogs were extremely excited. The gate began to drop, and Duke took the lead fast, literally pulling John over the top of it with him.

"Let's go! Let's go! Don't stop!" Tomahawk commanded.

John waded quickly through the waist-deep water as Duke and the other dogs swam along with their handlers. Bullets were kicking up the salty water all around them, and it seemed that death was imminent.

Smiles fell victim to a large wave, knocking him face first into the ocean.

"Come on, dammit! Move it! Let's go, Smiles!" yelled John. He had to keep everybody moving, or they'd surely be killed. He reached down and pulled Smiles up by the hair. Tomahawk and Brass ran up to assist.

"Get moving! Go! Go! Go!" Brass demanded.

"Sir, they got to get that pillbox! They're mowing us down! We can't make it up the hill!" a random marine yelled out, giving up hope.

"Dammit, son! Get back! That's an order! Now!" Tomahawk screamed. He needed to keep these men in check, and he knew it.

The marine turned to run but was struck in the chest by enemy fire. He and John made eye contact as he collapsed to the ground, instantly dying as the bullets ripped his chest apart, spraying blood on John. Suddenly everything became all too real for John.

"Holy shit, holy shit, holy shit. Go. Go! Across the road! Run! Run, dammit!" John shouted in a panicked voice. There was no time for him to think now—just react.

The battleship began to pound the pillboxes, eventually halting their deadly fire. Several marines on the hill cheered as the area by the pillbox was blown into the air by the hellish cannon explosions.

Back on the boat, the captain looked though some binoculars to see a marine with a flamethrower burning the pillbox to the ground.

In a ditch at the bottom of the ridge, the others were preparing for the fight of their lives.

"Dig in, boys! Get your holes dug! You'll be in the foxholes for some time. Stake your dog in by the creek. Keep your damn helmets on. Tomahawk, come with me. We're going to the CP. We need firepower. Keep up with me!" Brass ordered.

They turned and ran off up the creek bed, around the bend, and out of site. They needed the extra firepower and sought out the colonel at the command post. Without his permission for extra munitions, they didn't stand a chance.

"Foxholes. Dammit!" Gregory yelled.

The men started to separate for their task.

Brass and Tomahawk sprinted through some low-water rice paddies. Bullets flew overhead as they jumped into a hole inhabited by a dead marine. A sense of death hung in the air like a wool blanket.

"Son of a bitch! Let's go!" Brass commanded.

He snatched the dog tags from the mangled, life-less body. The dead marine's eyes stared through him as the dinky little chain snapped from around his neck. Tomahawk reached over and closed what was left of his eyes, realizing the impossible task of closing half an eyelid. It was melted off from the blast that he'd succumbed to.

Brass and Tomahawk finally reached the command post. Out of breath, they were greeted by Colonel Westinghouse. He granted their wishes but told them to bring their men along the riverbed and have them dig in at the command post. It was much safer, and it was sheltered from the shelling by the cliff. The two men weren't happy to turn back around but they obeyed without question. There was a reason he was a colonel. He had survived worse and knew best.

Brass and Tomahawk reached their men and broke the news—with mixed reactions from the marines. The men, tired from stress, digging, and running, slowly grabbed their gear and headed for their dogs.

"Move it! This isn't playtime, soldiers!" yelled Brass.

They ran past the dead marine they had passed before. Brass stopped everyone so they could see him clearly. He wanted to make sure that everybody got a good look at what could happen to them if they weren't at the top of their game.

"Take a look, boys."

They reached for their helmets and tightened their straps.

"Take a good long look. Be smart out here. Now let's get the hell out of here!" Brass said with urgency.

They all ran by, taking a look at the mangled body.

At the command post, the sun was falling as they dug more foxholes. Gregory slung his shovel down.

"Fuck this digging! How much dirt can we move?" Gregory complained.

"Keep digging, Gregory. You'll want to sleep in it," explained John.

A marine ran up to him.

"Gregory, I'll dig your hole if I can sleep in it tonight," the marine stated.

"What?" Gregory was confused.

"The dogs, they know when someone's trying to sneak into camp. I'll make it big enough for the three of us," the marine explained.

"Shit. Come dig mine," Ricci offered.

"Here's my shovel." Gregory handed him the shovel.

The marine took it and started to dig. Ricci turned to the other marines.

"Anyone want to sleep in a safe place tonight?" Ricci asked.

Several of the marines swiftly ran over. Brass, Colonel Westinghouse, and Tomahawk, who were making their rounds, walked over.

"I think it's safe to say our boys got some respect around here," Brass pointed out.

The evening gave way to the moonlight. It shone through the large palm trees and tropical foliage, casting shadows along the tree line. The shadows flickered and danced on the ground. The leaves blowing in the ocean breeze rubbed one another creating a mix of noises in the humid air. The tents at the command post filled with the salty air, breathing it in and allowing it to escape through the vented tops. The sounds of combat had been halted since the sun hid behind the horizon.

The men and dogs were exhausted and finally succumbed to their bodies' need for sleep. The moon hung high in the midnight sky and acted as God's night-light.

Duke was half-asleep. His servant mentality did not allow for him to completely let his guard down. John slept with his hand on Duke's throat, actually wrapped around him much like they had slept on the train. Something caught Duke's ear and his head darted up in suspicion, his nose soaking up the air for clues. He let out a deep, low growl that vibrated John's hand and snapped him back to reality. John opened his eyes slowly and reached for his gun. Duke jumped, and John yanked his leash just as the Japanese opened fire on them. A small group of Japanese had snuck in around their camp. He placed his gun over the edge of the foxhole and blindly pulled the trigger, hoping that the enemy didn't know they were invisible. Gregory jumped up from his slumber and grabbed Titan, who was now viciously pulling the leash. He yanked a grenade pin and tossed it. With the loud bang came several blood-curdling screams. Somehow the grenade had hit its target—and the men were shocked by just how close the Japanese were. The gunfire stopped.

"I think you got 'em!" John said.

"Go check it out!" Gregory pleaded.

"You go check it out! I'm going to toss another!" replied John.

He tossed another grenade out, and the thunderous burst shook the ground. John peeped his head over the edge, hoping and praying that he would see nothing but dead bodies.

"I see two! They look dead!" he said and kept staring.

"I'm glad I dug this hole for you," the marine was quick to point out.

"I'm going out!" John said bravely.

He ran, attempting to serpentine back and forth, making sure he wasn't an easy target to hit for anybody who might still be waiting.

He found the two dead soldiers lying on top of the third one. He grabbed Duke and was horrified by what he saw. It was then, in that moment, that he realized what Duke had just done. His dog had just saved their lives. He reached down and hugged Duke, and for perhaps the first time since the fighting began, he realized just how important to the fight man's best friend had become. Months of training were displayed in a matter of forty-five seconds.

The superiors were having a conversation inside Colonel Westinghouse's tent. The colonel explained a job that needed to be done and requested Duke for it. He was impressed with Duke.

"We've been hitting them hard, and they've been silent for a while. Maybe we got 'em. I don't know. You'll meet up with a small squad," explained Westinghouse.

"What will we have as far as firepower?" Brass asked.

A marine was firing up the flamethrower, giving it a quick test. Sergeant Ranch, a man of medium stature and build and missing his left ear from prior combat, loved pulling the trigger on that weapon. He loved fire. He loved watching it burst from the tip of the flamethrower.

"Son of bitch! That's hot as the sun! That'll melt your face right off. Gather up, let's move!" Ranch ordered as he looked over at their tent.

"Markle! Come see me!" Brass ordered.

John ran over.

"Markle, today is the day."

"What day is that, sir?"

"We're going to meet Sergeant Ranch. We're going up the ridge. Grab Duke."

"Yes, sir."

He turned and made a quick run over to Duke, a bit distraught.

"You ready, boy? We earn our stripes today," John explained to his friend.

"What was that about?" asked Gregory.

"I'm heading out. Up the ridge with Duke," John explained.

"Be careful."

"Let's go!" Brass barked out.

They slapped hands. He and Duke ran to meet Brass.

John, Duke, and Brass were walking up the jungle trail when they spotted the squad. They converged in a group of trees for shelter.

"Sergeant. Lieutenant Brass."

"Nice to see you, sir," Ranch replied.

He looked over to Duke.

"So, what do we do around the dog?" Ranch asked.

"Do you smell like a Jap?" Brass asked.

"No."

"Do you look like one?" Brass continued.

"No."

"Then you don't have anything to worry about." Brass smiled as they shook hands.

"We're going up the hill today. We're going to see if they're dead, and if not, then we will kill them. You have the flamethrower?" Brass asked.

"Hell, yes," Ranch replied with a grin.

"Good. Markle! Come over here," Brass yelled.

"Yes, sir."

"Meet Sergeant Ranch."

"Good afternoon, sir."

"Your dog's a good dog?" Ranch asked John.

"The best," was John's quick reply.

"Good. I just came from down the beach. Those sons of bitches on the cliff took out half a platoon down there. So I want to kill a few of them today. What do you say?" Ranch said.

"Good idea."

"You ready, Markle?" Brass asked.

"Yes, sir," John replied.

"Good. You're walking point. If shit gets heavy, throw both of these."

Brass tapped the two grenades hanging on John's vest.

"Take Private Marcus with you. When you get to the field south of the ridge, burn it. Burn it all. We need to clear a line of sight. We've got to clear a way up there. Failure is not an option," Brass explained.

Private Marcus was standing next to John with the flamethrower. They all turned and started up the wooded trail.

"Markle!" Brass called out.

John turned around.

"Trust his instincts," Brass said. He pointed to Duke.

"I trust his more than mine," John replied.

Marcus and John walked cautiously along the ridge trail. Duke suddenly stopped and alerted, pointing up and away. John instantly signaled to stop and get down. They scattered into the brush.

"Did he see something?" Marcus was quick to ask.

"Something's got him spooked. Stay here. We're gonna move up. When I whistle, come up. Stay low," John warned.

John and Duke slowly made their way out, crawling up the trail on their bellies. They took shelter about thirty yards up. Duke alerted. They hid as two Japanese soldiers slowly walked by. He grabbed Duke's snout. John looked to see but lost them in the jungle. He let out a deep breath. He whistled for Marcus, still maintaining his cover. Duke alerted in the opposite direction now.

"Dammit!" John said. He looked for Marcus. He saw him approaching cautiously just as the Japanese scouts were making their way back.

The Japanese soldiers stopped dead in their tracks and hit the ground. At the same time, Marcus was heading up the far side of the trail. He came into John's vision. He gave him the sign to take cover, that he had seen two of them.

Marcus immediately found cover behind a blown-up tree stump. John signaled that he was counting to three and then tossing his grenades. He tossed them and lay across Duke and then unloaded his rifle. He stopped when there was no return fire, and an eerie silence filled the air. He and Duke waited for a second, and then rolled out and cautiously made their way toward the area where he had thrown the grenades. There was no sign of the Japanese soldiers. Duke alerted once again, his paw off the ground and pointing. John hit the ground, only to fall upon a severed arm.

"Aw shit. Is that what you're smelling?" John asked.

He whistled for Marcus, who emerged from the bushes, still maintaining a cautious gait. Marcus was suddenly blasted with a rash of bullets, hitting him and digging up dirt all around his feet. He crawled back to the tree stump, not sure yet how badly he'd been hit. But when he reached down and felt the blood gushing from his chest, he knew that death was only seconds away.

He turned and opened fire.

"Stay down!" John warned Marcus.

He gave orders to Duke to stay as well. John turned and shimmied over to Marcus, who had perished due to his injuries.

"No. No. No. Dammit. Dammit," John said in anguish.

He took the flamethrower off Marcus and put it on. Duke watched his handler for instruction. He signaled to Duke to walk in the other direction. He did and soon took on fire from the Japanese. John used his companion as a decoy. Duke jumped into a shallow ditch, sheltering him from the bullets. John followed the enemy gunfire and got an eye on them and their small cave. He noticed a few marines coming up the trail. He motioned for them to stay down and to flank the position from the left. He continued to use Duke as a distraction. Finally, one of the marines made it around to the top of the cave and threw in a couple of grenades. No resistance appeared. John made his way to the cave and lit it up with the flamethrower. A few seconds later, out ran three Japanese on fire, flames pouring from the napalm stuck to their skin. The M1A1 flamethrower was the best they had and the latest model. It replaced the M1 model and began using napalm. It could shoot flames over forty yards with fifty percent accuracy where the M1 could shoot twenty yards with ten percent. It was a sight to see when it would shoot a flame forty yards and have it slash back and forth like a whip.

Two of the three had quickly succumbed to their injuries. Their screaming stopped when their vocal cords melted. John noticed one was still alive, missing half an arm. The burning Japanese soldier tried to scream but nothing came out. He clawed at John's boot. John pushed him away with his foot, ripping some of the soldier's melted skin off his face. John signaled for Duke, who came running back immediately.

"Don't shoot that son of a bitch. Let him burn," John yelled out. Suddenly this became personal, very personal. He wasn't about to let this murderer off so easily; he wanted him to suffer, and suffer severely. John felt numb inside, almost like his soul had just been yanked from his body, and there was nothing left in there but a hollow shell. He turned and lit up the cave one more time and then set the field ablaze.

Back at the command post the group, considered their losses.

"We lost three dogs in as many days out there in that jungle," Brass explained. The dogs were scattered all over parts of the island but news of one of their passing usually made its way around quickly.

"Sad," Tomahawk replied.

"Seven altogether now. For God's sake, they even made a cemetery for 'em." Brass was glad his canine marines were receiving an appropriate burial. The cemetery was built in a large rice patty field in Asan. Their grave markers were wooden crosses with their names written on them. The dogs were buried alongside other marines. Of the seven that had perished so far, six were killed in combat and one died from heartworms.

"Their sharpshooters are going for the dogs," Tomahawk explained.

"You make sure that all dogs are buried there. We retrieve their bodies at all costs, got it?" Brass asked.

"Sir, that goes without saying," replied Tomahawk.

John sat in a tent alone, sheltering himself from the rain. He pulled a letter from Tommy from his pocket and began to read. Duke was by his side.

"Hi, Private Markle. How is Duke? I hope you and him are doing good and being safe. Have you killed any Japs? I haven't got a letter from you in a while. Dad says that Duke is fine and there's nothing to worry about but I want to know for sure. Please write me back. Tommy."

He put the letter down and started to reflect on the day he'd just experienced. He broke down and began to weep profusely. He pulled out Emily's locket and rubbed her picture, as if somehow that would give him solace, but it didn't. The day brought with it so many new revelations about who he was and what he was becoming. He had burned a man alive for doing the same thing he was doing: following orders and fighting in a war. Could he really live with that? Would he? And he had also used Duke as bait, putting his new best friend in jeopardy and risking it all. These feelings of remorse and pain smashed into John's conscience and left him questioning the man he'd always thought he was. *But this was war,* he rationalized. It was kill or be killed, and he couldn't let the life of a dog, no matter how special that dog was, take precedence over the life of his fellow soldiers.

The next morning John and Duke were suddenly awakened by Lieutenant Brass screaming from afar.

"Markle, Gregory, O'Ryan! Get over here!" Brass yelled out.

They converged on him.

"How's everybody? Look, we're moving farther in. Grab your packs, and round up your dogs. Head over to the Willys. We're leaving in ten minutes," Brass announced.

He turned and walked away. They turned to see about twenty war-torn Willys jeeps in a row, ready to head out, many of them fitted with machine guns. The old jeeps had seen better days.

"Cowboy up," O'Ryan said.

"Damn. I was just getting comfortable," joked Gregory.

"At least we'll have some firepower." John was at least happy for that. A stretcher jeep pulled up, and a skinny Sergeant Mitch waved them over.

"Come on over here, guys. We got room for you and your dogs," he said as he took a swig from his canteen.

"Thanks. I'm John."

"Sergeant Mitch."

"Where we heading today?"

Mitch ignored the question.

"What the dog's name?" he asked instead.

"This is Duke. That's Gregory and Fever. That's O'Ryan and Raptor," John explained.

"Those sure are some bad-ass names," Mitch pointed out.

"They're some bad-ass dogs," O'Ryan added.

"They killed anyone yet?" Mitch asked. He spit his chew out of the jeep and left a stream of brown slimy spit hanging from his lips.

"That shit'll kill ya. I don't care what the doctors say," Gregory pointed out.

"Nah, boy. Them Japs will kill ya. This tobacco is the least of my worries. I've been up on that ridge already. Twice. It's bad up there. You can smell the dead. The burnt flesh, the rotten bodies, and those fucking flies. They're thick as smoke up there. Son of a bitch, here we go again. My advice: keep your helmet on," Mitch warned.

The pack of jeeps came to a sliding halt.

"Everybody out! Stay on the right!" Mitch ordered.

John and O'Ryan exited next to one another. John thought he needed to clear the air with O'Ryan about Emily. The last few days of war were weighing on his mind, and it could be now or never. He grabbed him and pulled him aside. O'Ryan was surprisingly open to talk. The war had had an effect on him. Most soldiers harden up as they encounter death repeatedly, but the opposite was true for O'Ryan. It had softened him up somewhat. O'Ryan explained that he and Emily had grown up together. Her father was abusive and an alcoholic. Her mother took her in the middle of the night and left him. A couple years later, her mother was diagnosed with brain cancer and died seven months later. Emily went to live with O'Ryan and his family—her aunt and uncle. She never heard from her father again.

They ended the conversation closer than they were before. O'Ryan, being O'Ryan, needed to have the last word. "You be the man she never had: her protector, her rock, her everything."

John let him have those last words. They resonated within his soul.

They walked back over and joined the group.

John stood next to a young and stuttering Private Hart.

"I-I-I'm going with you and that dog," Hart explained.

"What happened to you?" John was quick to ask.

"I have a s-stuttering p-problem," replied Hart.

"You don't say? The dog's name is Duke," he answered.

"Hi, D-Duke."

"Markle, you're going with the third platoon," Brass commanded.

Hart smiled.

"Let me guess. You're in the third?" John asked.

"You're d-damn s-skippy I am," replied Hart.

"Gregory! You're with second. Everyone get your shit together. We leave in fifteen minutes," Brass ordered.

John, Hart, Duke, and several other marines were slowly making their way up a winding trail, surrounded by the burnt-grass fields.

"All right, boys. The first division has cleared us a good path. Word is there is a POW camp up on the north side of the ridge. We're going there. We may encounter pockets of resistance, so be prepared. Markle, take Hart with you," Tomahawk ordered.

Private Hart smiled. John walked over to Tomahawk.

"Sir, with all due respect, I don't think Hart is right for this mission. I mean look at him." John glanced over at Hart, who was still smiling and looking up to the sky.

"Markle, I know he doesn't look like much but he's a deadeye with that rifle. He scored top marks. You may need him up there."

"But, sir, I need heavy fire with me, not a stuttering sniper."

"Take Private Drake, too. Make it work, Markle," ordered Tomahawk.

John, Duke, Drake, and Hart headed up the trail. They made their way cautiously until they opted to take a rest. They ventured off the trail to a more secluded area.

"So who's a baseball fan?" Drake asked, trying to lighten things up a bit.

"I-I am," Hart stuttered.

"Who's your team?" asked Drake.

"The Saint Louis B-Browns," replied Hart.

"My least favorite team. What about you, Markle?"

"I don't really follow baseball, but I would go with the Cards."

"Ding-ding! We have a winner," Drake said as he smiled.

"What about you?" Markle asked.

"Shit man, Cards all the way. I'm from St. Louis," Drake replied.

"So why aren't y-you a B-B-Browns fan?" asked Hart.

"I was playing for the Cards just a year ago," said Drake. "Fuckin' draft got me. I mean, I was working in a factory and playing ball. So I'm ready to get this war over with and get back to the States and win a world series. Besides, the Browns suck."

"T-they are kickin' t-tail this year," Hart was quick to add.

"Me and Duke are going to head up the trail a ways. Let's go, boy," said John.

Duke hopped up and immediately alerted.

"Down," ordered John.

"W-what's he doing?" Hart asked.

"Shut up," John responded.

Drake readied his machine gun. Two Japanese soldiers appeared in the distance.

"I can get them," Hart said.

"You can hit them from here?" John pointed out.

"I c-can hit one of them for s-sure." He peered through his sights and contemplated getting both of them with one shot. "Maybe even both of them," he added.

"Do it. Drake, get ready to light them up. Duke, down, down," John ordered.

He pulled Duke down below some old fallen trees.

"Get ready," John said softly. He finished penning a note to Brass and attached it to Duke. Messenger duty was the only weak spot on Duke's impressive résumé.

The hope was that he would deliver the note to Brass and inform him of the impending enemy on the hill. Duke had delivered the most important note during training, the one to Emily in the middle of the night that resulted in their first kiss, so John was confident in Duke's ability to reach Brass.

Hart took aim and waited for the two Japanese soldiers to stand one in front of the other. He took aim on the lead soldier's neckline and pulled the trigger, hitting the first one in the neck and allowing the bullet to penetrate and hit the second soldier in the neck as well. They both dropped immediately.

"Son of a b-bitch. I g-got both of those f-fuckers!" Hart yelled.

A third Japanese soldier took off running. John released Duke.

"Take it back, boy. Run! Run!" John yelled.

Duke took off down the trail, understanding his orders. About midway through, he stopped in his tracks at the sound of a screaming woman. At the edge of the trail, hiding in what was once tall grass, was a Chamorro family. They too sat still and stared at Duke staring at them. Duke slowly and cautiously walked toward them. He cocked his head in curiosity. He made his way up to them and sat down. In one side of his pouch was a canteen full of water and some food rations. The family appeared malnourished and wounded. A younger lady was in the middle of giving birth, agonizing in pain. They were hesitant to reach into Duke's pouch at first, but his demeanor finally put them at ease when he lifted up his right paw as if to shake. Suddenly he didn't look so frightful. They got the canteen and passed it around, paying special attention to the pregnant girl to ensure she was taken care of. After a few more minutes, Duke continued his trek back to camp to deliver the note.

Duke came running into camp and went straight to Lieutenant Brass.

"What the hell are you doing here?" Brass asked the dog.

He reached down into the messenger pouch and retrieved the letter.

"Up on the north side of the trail. Small resistance. Trail is cleared all the way to us," he read out loud. He reached down and petted Duke. "Good boy."

Duke, Brass, and the other marines headed up the trail, and Duke led them to the Chamorro family. The young lady was in the middle of giving birth. She was screaming in pain.

"For Christ's sake! Medic! Get the medic over here," Brass yelled out.

"Yes, sir?" the medic replied as he hurried over.

"What do you mean, 'Yes, sir'? Get over there and help her!" Brass yelled.

"Get me some towels and water!" the medic requested.

He ran over to the girl and began assessing the situation while Duke sat by patiently. A few moments later, her baby was finally born. The medic was cradling the newborn as another cleaned the baby off. Then the medic handed the baby to its mother. Seconds later, five more Chamorro emerged from the jungle's edge.

"You two. Go up and get the scout group. This just turned into a humanitarian mission," Brass explained.

The marines watched the Chamorro interact with one another. John and Duke got up and walked out to the ten-year-old Chamorro child. He had bandages around his arm and head. The Chamorro were curious about the marines, but were even more intrigued by the dogs. They smiled at the dogs, who were doing tricks.

"Hi, I'm John. What's your name?" he asked the child.

The child didn't really understand English, but he was not a shy child, and he understood John's body language. He smiled.

"I bet these poor people haven't smiled in a long time," John said in a sad tone.

"Well, today, it feels good to help people rather than kill 'em. It's terrible. I mean look at the scars on that kid. Looks like they poked him with burning sticks," Brass pointed out.

"It was their gun barrels. Let me and Duke go up the hill," John requested.

"Okay," replied Brass.

"I need Hart as well. That stuttering son of a bitch killed two Japs with one shot. Honest truth," John explained.

Hart, John, Duke, Gregory, Fever, and a few others were making their way up the trail. It was intense as they came upon the site where Hart had shot the two Japs. John gave a signal to stop and get down. There were two more of the enemy circling about fifty yards away. Hart took aim. He had one lined up when a gunshot rang out before he could squeeze his trigger. Fever hit the ground hard and yelped. The sniper had hit his target.

"Fever!" Gregory yelled.

They opened fire. Gregory grabbed Fever and pulled him to safety, risking his own life to pull his canine companion from danger. Fever was in bad shape. He knew that, but Fever didn't. He still tried to get back to his feet and fight and protect his master. But with every move, the blood loss worsened, jetting from his gunshot wound. The bullet had entered into his chest and made its way out by his hip, shattering the bone and fragmenting it internally.

Fever struggled to move but finally found comfort in remaining still. His panting increased, as did the blood coming from his mouth. It meant his lungs were filling with blood, and he didn't have long.

"Dammit!" Gregory wept.

The mortar shells filled the air as the machine guns ripped through the jungle like small missiles.

"Come on boy, come on boy! Don't die on me! Don't die on me." Gregory pleaded as he plunged a cloth into the gaping wound. All his attention was on Fever.

He held him in his arms. Both were covered in blood. Fever took a deep breath and blood spurted from his mouth. Gregory positioned himself right in front of Fever's face. He realized that his friend was not going to make it. As the sounds of mortars and gunshots faded out, he focused on his last moments with his best friend, moments that would remain with him long after his return stateside.

"I love you, buddy. I sure do. I'm sorry. I'm so sorry," he said, with tears in his eyes, running out and down his cheeks.

Fever took his last breath, and his body went limp in Gregory's arms. His tears fell to the ground, mixing with Fever's blood. Gregory held his friend and looked to the sky. Blood covered his body. His eyes moved away from sorrow, and instead of filling with more tears, they began to fill with rage. He set Fever's body to the side, stood up, and started firing as fast as his carbine rifle could. He threw caution to the wind and bullets in the air.

"Fever!" Gregory screamed out over the roar of the gunshots.

"We've been ambushed! We need to pull back! Pull back! Dammit!" John yelled.

Private Gregory scooped up his best friend's body and ran toward the east side of the path, crossing it, and disappearing into the thick jungle.

They buried Fever the following day at the cemetery. Lieutenant Brass addressed the marines at the funeral.

"There are too many crosses in this cemetery. Nine. Nine crosses. Nine dogs. Marines, we need to ensure that our brave and most loyal companions are forever with us. They know not what they fight for, but they do know they fight with us. Fever was an excellent dog, a great marine, and the best companion one could ask for. His loyalty was unquestionable from day one. His nerves unshakable and his character incomparable. He was a war dog. A devil dog. A marine. May he rest in peace, knowing that he unselfishly perished for his loyal companion. Godspeed, Fever."

John made his way over to his friend.

"You all right?" John asked Gregory, sure that he wasn't.

"I've never had anyone around me, like family or anything, die. I'm fuckin' angry. I'm sad. I don't know."

"He was a good dog. You gave him some peace while he passed." John was trying to make Gregory feel better, but it wasn't working.

John patted him on the back empathically. He was sad for his friend, and he knew he didn't want the same fate for Duke.

14

LOSING FRIENDS

Emily sat in her favorite spot by the window and read the latest letter from John. She feared these letters, never knowing what was going to be said. She always had a sense of ease when she saw his handwriting on the envelope. It was better to be addressed by him than by the marines and the US government.

"We lost Fever today. A sniper got him. He was the ninth dog since we got here. Gregory is pretty bad. I can't blame him. I would be too. I miss you. I'm ready to come home. I love you. Sorry this letter is so short. Write back soon."

She took the letter and stuck it into a box with the other letters. The box was full. She gazed down at a picture of John with Duke and began to sob as she blew out a candle.

2

The hot summer sun beat down on them as their platoon took a pounding with intense mortar fire in the heat of Guam's jungle. Bullets flew past the group, ripping through the thick, humid air.

"Dammit! Get moving! Get moving!" Brass blurted out.

"Sir! We need to push up over the ridge!" Tomahawk said.

"Shit! I know I know! Grab some men and head north! Keep the flank and stay off the trail!" replied Brass.

"Yes, sir!"

"You crazy son of a bitch. Be careful. Private! Fill the air with shells! Let's kill these kamikaze bastards!" Brass commanded.

This battle was quick and ended just as fast as it started. Air support peppered the ground from above, eventually killing the Japanese and dismantling their equipment. The platoon moved in to examine the destruction and look for survivors. A few Japanese ran into the jungle, but before they departed they sliced their captives up, leaving their bodies as evidence of their cruelty and savage warfare. They came upon the camp hidden in the foliage. It was a prisoner-of-war camp. There were no prisoners left alive.

Tomahawk, along with several marines, cautiously approached the Japanese POW camp. They took cover in the brush as Smiles, John, and Private Davis scouted the camp with their dogs. Parts of the camp were still smoldering as they made their way around it. The little bamboo huts housed a few cots and baskets of rice. Inside many of the makeshift cages were the bodies of several Chamorro.

"Oh my God," John said.

"Whatcha got?" Smiles asked.

Smiles saw the mangled torsos of several women. The sight of it was more than he could take, and he spewed his breakfast on the dirt path. It was a horrible sight.

"Holy shit. They cut the babies from them," Smiles said in disbelief and with a shaky voice. He continued to gag, and after taking a few deep cleansing breaths, his sickness quickly turned to rage. All the men were in shock at the brutality of the enemies. Smiles, ripe with anger now, wiped the vomit from his lips and began to sprint to the jungle's edge, but Tomahawk nearly clotheslined him, stopping him from almost certain death. Smiles's eyes were dead with a thousand-yard stare. He had lost it. A few guys tried to get his attention, but his mind was somewhere else, lost in thought, conflicted in emotion. He had reached his breaking point. The skinny kid with thick glasses gripped his rifle tight, his bottom lip quivering in anger as he glanced around the camp, fixated on the mutilated corpses of the natives he was there to save.

Smiles yelled and fired several shots into the jungle without a care of where the bullets were going, many flying over his platoon's heads. They hit the ground quickly, dodging their companion's outburst of firepower. They yelled out to him to stop, but he wasn't and didn't until his clip ran dry. He then screamed out as he ran over and kicked the body of a dead Japanese soldier over and over again. He kicked and kicked at it, eventually smashing the side of its head. The body rolled to its side. There was a click sound, and a live grenade tumbled from behind the body. They saw it roll around, and within seconds it stopped moving. They turned to flee but the body exploded at Smiles's feet, sending him somersaulting into the air. The explosion was so violent that the force also tossed Blade. Enemy fire began to rain down on them once again, causing pure pandemonium. The explosion was the Imperial soldiers' signal to open fire. Their booby trap was triggered. The bullets zoomed past their heads, splitting the thick trunks of the palm trees and ripping their leaves to smithereens. The sandy loam soil kicked up dirt and debris as the shells rammed into the earth with unforgiving force.

Smiles was still lying on the ground in shock and gazing up at sky. He shivered and shook from the trauma. He managed to glance toward his legs. They were severed from the blast, but he was unable to tell. But he knew, even amid his shock, that something was terribly wrong. Blade quickly regained consciousness and ran over to Smiles's side. His faithful companion jumped into action, instinctively grabbing Smiles by the jacket and attempting to drag him to safety. John and the others ran over to give Blade a hand. They pulled him to safety over a small ridge. Only by the grace of God did they elude the cascade of gunfire.

"Get me some bandages! Give me something!" ordered John. He was given some dressings and quickly tried to stop the bleeding, but it seemed impossible. The wounds were just too gaping and horrific, and the blood flowed, unstoppable. Smiles's legs were missing from the middle of his thighs down, his flesh stretched and burnt from the powder and shrapnel. The corroded artery gushed bright-red blood, soaking the dirt and staining it black with death. The blood was leaving his body fast, and he was beginning to lose consciousness. The bullets continued to fly over their heads, severing the tree branches and causing them to fall onto the group of marines.

"Smiles! Smiles! Stay with us, buddy, come on! Come on! Dammit! Smiles!" John yelled out as he desperately tried to stop the bleeding and keep his friend among the living.

Blade just sat next to them, stoic in his manner, as the shock of the day was still hanging over him like the enemy it was. Duke just sat there too. The dogs knew how serious the situation was and obeyed their handlers.

"Come on, Smiles! We need you, buddy. Who's gonna play the bugle for us?" John teased.

"I'm cold," Smiles mumbled. "And my legs! Where's my legs?" Smiles tried to look down again. In his confused mind he knew something was wrong, very wrong, and his eyes showed it.

"Don't look. Don't look. You'll be all right," John said, trying to comfort his dying friend. Smiles wasn't going to be all right, and they all knew it. His injuries were simply too severe.

John covered him up, making sure to cover all of his lower half.

"Are we winning? Did we win?" Smiles asked.

He reached over and started to pet Blade. Blade lay down next to him, giving him some great comfort.

"We won, buddy, we won. You won," replied John.

Private Smiles took a deep breath, exhaled, and slipped away. His dead man's stare from earlier left, and his eyes now had a peaceful, serene gaze. His arms were wrapped around Blade. John just hung his head as he watched his good friend pass.

"Dammit. We've been over it a million times. Don't fuck with the bodies! Don't touch the bodies! Let the bodies lie and rot where you find them. Dammit!" Tomahawk ranted, feeling the frustration of such a senseless death.

Luckily, a small group of marines emerged from the tree line a hundred yards away and engaged the enemy, eventually halting their advance. Between Brass's group and the other company flanking the opposition, the enemy soldiers were all eventually killed.

After the gun smoke was lifted away by the salty, humid air, a small group of Chamorro emerged. They cautiously walked up to John and placed their hands on him. One of the Chamorro spoke in very broken English. He was humble and spoke softly.

"He died for us," the Chamorro man whimpered, clearly touched by what had just happened.

"He died for all of us," John corrected. "All of us!"

He wiped a tear from his eye and covered Smiles's face with a blanket. His soul was hurt, injured just as much as Smiles's broken body. He held his friend's hand, unable to leave. Brass eventually had to comfort him and get him to let go so they could get his body back to camp.

At the command post, Brass sat and wrote a letter to Smiles's family. The thunder shook the ground as the lightning lit up the cloud-covered Pacific sky. He despised writing these letters and struggled for just the right words that might bring some comfort and understanding. But what might those words be? Did they even exist?

"What do you suppose we do?" Tomahawk asked. He sat by the window, watching the lightning streak across the sky.

"For starters, we stop letting our dogs and men get killed. We have orders to leave for Agana in the morning. We'll be meeting up with the 3rd War Dog Platoon and scout the five-mile line. We will be leading on every advancing point."

Tomahawk, who liked to reflect on his Indian culture, told Brass a story that night, a story about the thunderbird. Although Brass didn't always like to hear his stories, believing many of them to be the result of peyote-induced visions, he opted to hear him out this time.

"The thunderbird is a legendary creature with great power and supernatural strength. The Sioux called them the *Wakinyan,* meaning 'sacred wings.' The legend says these large birds create storms when they flap their enormous wings. Thunder is created when they fly, and the clouds pull together and push away as the wind moves about their wings, sometimes creating tornados. Lightning shoots from their eyes when they blink."

He went on to describe how the thunderbird defended the defenseless creatures of the sea when a great whale was killing all the other whales for sport, selfishness, and hatred. The thunderbird eventually lifted the whale from the ocean, taking him a mile in the air and dropping him to the earth. Not only did the giant bird protect those that could not protect themselves, he also brought rain with him as his wings flapped and his eyes blinked. He brought protection and live-saving rain, which always made things greener and healthier.

After listening to the story, which captured his attention, Brass asked, "and what kind of bird is this thunderbird?"

Tomahawk stared at him and confidently replied, "A big fuckin' bald eagle."

Brass quickly drew upon the symbolism of the story, shaking his head in agreement.

The marines made their way to Agana over the next few days, eventually getting there by late July. The 77th Infantry Division had a hard landing there, suffering the loss of lives and much-needed equipment. The handlers and their dogs were needed now more than ever. The Japanese had used the Chamorro to dig caves into the cliffs and hidden caves within the confines of the dense jungle. The caves were hard to find, and canine marines' noses were the best tool they had to help uncover them. John and the others had been on many missions since their arrival in Agana. Most were boring and without confrontation with the enemy. Still, they all knew danger was everywhere.

"Can you believe the Seabees already have the runway open?" John exclaimed with enthusiasm.

The Seabees were the construction division of the armed forces. They were tasked with building and repairing runways on the island. They also built shelters for the natives, much-needed safe havens for the innocent inhabitants of the lush island.

"We'll have some heavy air support. The word is that all the Japs have retreated," Ricci responded.

"Once again, we go in to find the stragglers," John said.

Lieutenant Brass walked by them as they spoke and wanted to make sure everybody knew how serious things were now.

"Shut it. We are heading up through Asan Point. If the war hasn't hit you yet, then just wait."

"For what, sir?" John asked, not sure he wanted to hear the answer—which never came anyway. What else they could possibly be exposed to?

They walked upon some old rice paddies and began to notice a line of white crosses that seemed to multiply as their approach angle changed. Many of the crosses still maintained their white luster from the fresh paint, evidence that death was always around the corner. Pine boxes sat off to the side, stacked next to each other, each waiting for burial and their own white cross.

"Christ. And we're winning this war?" Gregory couldn't believe what he saw.

"Keep a move on, men," barked Brass, who was not in the mood for sarcasm.

John looked over and saw the name JAMES SMILES written on one of the boxes. His heart dropped, and his mind filled with a sudden attack of remorse and frustration.

There were massive craters and flattened buildings; total destruction was everywhere. As the marines entered a demolished Agana, they couldn't help but feel the pain that must have been suffered there. There were massive amounts of debris littering the streets—and body parts everywhere. Craters from explosions pockmarked the streets and surrounding land. It looked like the end of the world. Brass walked up to Lieutenant Douglas, a slender young marine and leader of the 3rd War Dog Platoon.

"Good afternoon, sir," Brass said.

"And to you. My dogs have found nine mines swept to the roadside," Douglas answered.

"Impressive."

"Indeed," Douglas said with a grin.

"Word is we are taking the road to Yona together?" Brass asked.

"I've heard the same," Douglas responded.

"The other word is that you have been doing an outstanding job, Douglas. I'm glad to be a part of this."

"Tell me that again when we're back in the States," Douglas replied. "And those dogs you buried along the way? We're going to bring them here and bury them."

They patted each other on the back and parted ways to their platoons.

"Oh, Brass. When we get to Yona, have all your dogs checked. Heart worms are getting as bad as the Japs," Douglas warned.

They arrived at Yona a day later. Yona was a farming community of maybe twenty square miles and was inhabited by the Chamorro natives prior to the Imperial invasion. It was located on the eastern side of the island, above the cliffs of Pago Bay. The once-peaceful village was basically one large prison camp used to house the natives, mainly those from the north. They called the camp "Menenggon." The village was secured prior to their arrival, but the aftermath remained. Many of the Chamorro were killed by the Japanese soldiers once the marines entered the village. Despite the smoldering huts and houses, the abundant hibiscus flowers peppered the landscape, creating a red, yellow, and orange hue along the cliffside.

The soldiers were exhausted after the trip there. John was sitting in the latrine when Gregory knocked loudly on the door. It startled him.

"Whatcha doin' in there, boy?" Gregory asked.

"Taking a shit," John groaned.

"You sure about that?"

"I'm thinking about your mom."

"I heard we lost two more dogs today. And two just died from heartworms. And we're being absorbed into the MPC," Gregory added.

"The military police? Shit!" John didn't like the sound of that.

"Looks like more patrols for us," Gregory pointed out.

"Both the second and third?"

"Both of us. We'll all be together," Gregory explained.

They finished their conversation over a few shots of whiskey, a treat that Smiles had left behind for them. They toasted their fallen friend, clinking their glasses together and raising them in the air.

Gregory had something else on his mind. He told John a patrol had found O'Ryan in the jungle, hanging from a large ironwood pine tree. He had taken his own life, apparently. O'Ryan was a tough young man, but the war got the best of him. It disturbed John. He wondered if Emily knew—and if not, would he be the one to tell her about her cousin? He didn't want to be the one to break that news to her, much less lie and say he died fighting. John had his own thoughts. He reflected on his father's words that a coward dies a thousand deaths and a soldier dies but one. He was sure he wouldn't be the one to break the news, but if he was he would tell her the truth. Gregory agreed with his philosophy.

They both shook their heads and took one more drink, toasting O'Ryan and their friendship.

A few tents down, Brass, Douglas, and a stern, bald Major Tomball sat around having a few drinks and talking. Major Tomball was frustrated with the new assignment. It wasn't that he didn't like dogs, but he wasn't sure yet how they really figured into the equation. In fact, he wasn't at all sure yet whether or not they were an asset or a liability. After all, the men had enough to think about just trying to stay alive. They didn't need the added distraction of man's best friend. Tomball was at least sure of that much.

"Son of a bitch. Now I got to deal with a bunch of mutts too? How in the hell did this get on me? Are you behind this, Douglas?" Tomball asked in a pissy tone.

"No sir. Not at all. But we are happy to be a part of the MP. Our dogs bring a lot of value to the group," Douglas reassured.

"And now it's going to smell like a urine-soaked, shit-filled kennel around here," griped Tomball.

"Oh no, sir. We handle the shit," Brass was quick to point out.

"And what about all the dog piss?" Tomball asked.

"Sir, these dogs only shit when we tell them to shit. They only bark when we tell them to bark. We take care of our dogs," Douglas said with pride.

"All right, all right. Dammit. Listen, I know about the dogs. I've heard the stories. I know. I understand. I'm frustrated here. We're getting pockets of Japs, stragglers, and small squads, whatever. We need some help. How many dogs do you have right now?" asked Tomball.

"Between both platoons, healthy and ready to work, about forty. Have about ten that need attention," Brass responded.

"That's good. We're gonna start using all of 'em," barked Tomball.

"All right. We can have most of them healthy and ready in five days," promised Brass.

"Patrols start in forty-eight hours. Have them ready. We're not burning the midnight oil here. We're trying to win a war," grunted Tomball.

"Sir, a couple of them can't be ready that soon. They can barely walk," Douglas explained.

"I'm going to need both of you in the field working a dog. We are going to be rotating patrols. Two days out, two days in," Tomball continued.

"Yes, sir," responded Brass.

"Sir, and thank you for your continuous supply of medical equipment. I trust I will have everything I need to attend to the wounded?" Douglas asked.

"Indeed," Tomball responded.

John was sleeping comfortably in a small, open-sided tent when Gregory snuck in. The daily rain shower, not as torrential as usual, lightly pelted the top of the canvas covering. The afternoon showers were a welcome thing. They cooled the air just a bit until they passed, but then the humidity would rise to an unbearable level. At times it felt like breathing underwater.

"I sure do miss Smiles playing that damn bugle," he whispered.

There was no response from John, so Gregory spoke up a little louder. Clearly John was sound asleep.

"I miss Smiles playing that damn bugle," Gregory said in a louder tone, which instantly woke up John.

"How long you been sitting there?" John whispered, still half-asleep and wondering what Gregory was doing by his bunk.

"A few minutes. Just felt like talking." Gregory was a big guy, bigger than most of the marines. There was something very humbling to hear a man of his stature speak like that.

John looked over to see a letter from Emily with her lipstick kiss on it. There was also a letter from Tommy. He took a deep breath and smiled.

"I miss a lot of things too," he said as he sat up to help reassure his friend. His mind drifted from the dream Gregory had just disrupted.

The two men talked for a few more minutes, mainly about Smiles and how his family must have felt when they got the death notification. Gregory left to go to the latrine. John laid his head down on the pillow, and within minutes, he was back in dreamland again where Emily was waiting in the jungle for him.

She appeared angelic. The enemy was shooting all around as she hovered slightly above the ground. The bullets and debris flew through the air in slow motion when close to her.

She looked around as the gunfire increased and the enemy voices got louder. Her eyes, bright white with blinding rays of light, cast shadows in the smoky air.

"Run, John. Run now. Don't stop until you find Duke," she said with great urgency.

"Emily! Emily!" John cried out as he reached for her.

She faded away as she pointed in the direction of her beaming eyes. He turned to run full speed, dodging bullets, thorns, and tree branches. He leapt over a log and saw Duke, facing away, with his head down in the grass.

"Duke. Duke! Come here!" John called out to him.

Duke turned around and had blood all over his snout. He turned back around to continue eating, ignoring John and his commands. John slowly approached. He reached out to touch Duke, but the canine lunged at him, growling and snarling as if he were possessed, a true devil dog. John peered over the dog and saw that he was eating the bloody, swollen torso of Private Smiles. John jumped back and fell to the ground out of panic and disgust. He tried to get up, but the earth was now quicksand and swallowing him slowly, more and more each time he moved. Brass appeared and offered his hand, but when John reached for his hand, Brass just laughed in a deep, hollow, sinister voice. He then put his foot on John's head and slowly began to push him under the swallowing mixture of water and mud. John fought the earth but was unable to break free. Duke sat next to Brass, snarling and licking the blood from his snout. Over Brass's shoulder, he could see O'Ryan hanging from an apple tree, fighting the rope that was strangling him. In the blink of John's eye, the rope transformed into a snake and began to eat O'Ryan. The serpent's jaw made a loud pop as it dislocated and began to engulf O'Ryan headfirst, helmet and all.

John jumped up in his bed, realizing he was dreaming. Someone was playing the bugle in the background in an attempt to wake up the camp. He held Duke and grabbed onto Emily's locket tightly, his heart beating out of his chest.

15

BAD FEELINGS

The mist from a passing thunderstorm cast a rainbow across the sky on the morning of August 9, 1944. The glow from the sun reflecting from the fine drops of water made the rainbow appear to dance and twinkle. John and Duke were up front, walking point with one of the marines. They were startled by a rash of distant gunshots, followed by a few explosions.

John looked up at the rainbow overhead.

"I have a bad feeling about today," John shared.

"I suggest you lose that feeling. Get Duke over there," Brass suggested.

He pointed over to some abandoned huts.

"Something's not right," John said, feeling more uneasy than usual.

R. J. NEVENS JR.

"I told you to lose that attitude, Private. Keep walking," Brass ordered. His intuition was buzzing now as well.

In another part of the jungle, east of their location, Ricci and Titan ran for cover from a Japanese ambush. They were under heavy fire. They were out scouting a cave the natives had mentioned earlier. The Japanese soldiers would use the natives to dig out the caves and create a hidden tunnel system. Once they were finished, the locals were usually shot, beheaded, or sent off for more manual labor.

"Come on, boy! Run! Run! Run!" Ricci implored.

Ricci was suddenly struck down by a bullet and thrown in the air by an explosion. The world went silent as he flew into the trunk of a large palm tree. Titan was tossed into the nearby brush. Ricci was barely holding on to life as his eyes searched for Titan. His vision was fading into red as blood filled the corners of his eyes. The bullet had cut through his chest, exiting his upper back through his shoulder blade. He had sustained a massive head wound from the shrapnel and from smashing his head on the tree. He was clinging to life, slowly realizing his fate was upon him.

Three Japanese soldiers emerged from the dense forest. They cautiously approached and stood over him, their shadows casting shade on his face. It felt cool to him, blocking the harsh rays of the Pacific sun. They smiled at the sight of Ricci's demise. One leaned down and attempted to cut off his ear. The cold steel blade began to penetrate his cartilage as his warm blood crept from his skin. This sensation gave Ricci one last push. In a flash, Ricci pulled out his pistol, shot him in the head, and shot the other in his chest. The third soldier tried desperately to get his rifle pointed at Ricci, fumbling his weapon. Ricci hesitated to pull the trigger. The young Japanese soldier's eyes filled with dread as he saw his two comrades dead in a pool of their own blood. He held his hands up to surrender. Ricci, lying on his back and on his deathbed, lowered his weapon, willing to let his enemy walk away. A Japanese soldier surrendering was not normal.

"Why?" Ricci yelled at him, questioning why they hated each other so much that they would rather kill one another than be friends. "Why? Why do you hate us? Why do we hate you? Fuck!"

Blood ran from the corner of his mouth, flowing more heavily now. The head wound bled profusely. The skin from his scalp was folded to one side, and his face was covered in blood. He was barely recognizable.

"I don't want to kill anyone anymore. I don't!" Ricci was torn. His enemy just stood there, not understanding the words, but he did have an understanding that this marine was suffering with this war and what it had made of him. "Come here. Come here!" said Ricci.

The Japanese soldier just stood there.

"I said get the fuck down here!" Ricci raised his gun. "I want you to pray with me. I'm fucking dying here!" Ricci placed his hands together, giving the common hand signal for prayer. His enemy realized what he was asking. He was hesitant, but Ricci kept pushing him to come closer. He took a couple of steps toward Ricci. Their eyes met, cutting through the smoke of the battlefield and through their individual aggressions, cutting a direct line to their individual souls. The crow's-feet in their young eyes relaxed, hinting at a moment of understanding and empathy.

The beginning of a peaceful moment with the opposition was cut short when Titan leaped from the brush and latched onto the Japanese soldier's neck. The soldier thrashed around for a few seconds and managed to stab Titan twice in the side, puncturing his lung. The steel blade penetrated deep, but Titan didn't let go and held his bite tight.

His tenacious grip broke the soldier's windpipe eventually. Ricci and the Japanese soldier locked eyes as Titan finally let go when he sensed the enemy was dead. Ricci's eyes turned to sorrow. Titan limped over to Ricci. His front paw was severely damaged. That, along with the stab wounds, proved too much. They were able to comfort each other in their last moments. Ricci said a prayer as life slipped away from both of them. They died in each other's arms that day as marines, always faithful to one another.

At the same time, Private Gregory, Raptor, and a few other marines walked through thick jungle foliage. The daily mist from the overhead clouds rested on the large leaves that occasionally bounced into their faces when disturbed. They came to an opening overlooking the area where Ricci and Titan lay dead. They saw the land smoldering from the explosions and knew they needed to take a closer look.

"Hand me your specs," requested Gregory.

He peered through the dirty, scratched lenses and pulled them away quickly. He looked one more time. He pulled them down and hung his head. It was the last thing he wanted or expected to see.

"What?" the marine asked, sure he didn't want to know.

Gregory handed him the binoculars.

"Oh man. Is that Ricci?"

"And Titan. Dammit. Come on. We're going to go get them," Gregory said.

"Keep your heads on a swivel, men," another marine barked out.

An old, tattered American flag swayed in the wind as John, Duke, and the other marines approached the huts, many partially destroyed. They moved with caution as Duke led the way.

"Don't forget men, we're saving Americans here," John explained.

The group took shelter behind a blasted old rock wall, taking a needed rest-and-water break. Brass, taking advantage of the view, looked through the binoculars.

"See anything?" John asked.

"The trees over there. There's three of them. Here, take a look. I've been fighting these bastards for a while now. I can spot 'em a mile away. Sneaky little fucks. Get your gun—hurry," urged Brass.

He threw the binoculars back to John and took careful aim. They shot at the tree, killing two, but the third fell and then ran away.

"I'm going after him. Let's go, Duke!" And with that, John and Duke gave chase.

"Stop!" Brass yelled out.

John and Duke sprinted through the jungle but quickly lost track of the Japanese soldier. They continued to advance, sneaking through the dense foliage at a much slower pace. Duke stopped and alerted. His perfectly cropped ears rotated back and forth, listening for anything. John dropped to the ground. He signaled, and Duke ran back to his side. John looked through the jungle but couldn't see anyone.

After a few seconds, the Japanese soldier stood up, slowly making eye contact with John, who pointed his rifle right at him. Then a few other soldiers emerged from the jungle from behind the trees and up from the ground. An eerie feeling filled the air. The native birds were suddenly quiet. Their constant chirping and singing left the air, leaving only the wind shuffling the leaves on the trees. Noticing they appeared desperate and unarmed, perhaps deserters or just caught out in the open, John cautiously walked out and stood among the ten Japanese. The situation was tense as they stared each other down, not sure yet what the other was going to do. Duke stood his ground and growled, exposing those large, white teeth.

One of the Japanese smiled as he tossed a grenade right at them. John quickly shot him and one other soldier just before he turned to run. Duke turned as well just as the grenade exploded, sending them both flying. That one grenade seemed like the force of ten when it detonated. The blast twisted John's limbs as he soared through the air.

The other marines heard the explosion and quickly ran toward them. When they reached John and Duke, they laid down heavy fire on the Japanese, killing all of them. They hurried over to render aid. John was unconscious and injured, and Duke was lying on the ground a few feet away. Duke wasn't moving. After some prompting and smelling salts, John woke up, bewildered and bleeding.

"Oh man. What? I can't hear anything!" he said.

"You're all right. Sit back. Let's look at you." One of the marines took a closer look at him.

"Where's Duke?" John was quick to ask.

"Your arm is bad. We got to get you back," the marine explained.

"What? I said, where's my dog?"

"You're bleeding from the right ear too," Brass said, trying to keep the conversation off Duke.

They continued to hold bandages on his wounds as they carried him off. John continued to question them about the whereabouts of his dog, but he spotted Duke as they loaded him onto a stretcher. His physical pain was bearable to an extent, compared to his emotion reaction when he saw Duke not moving and gasping for breath. He cried out to his friend, reaching for him as his wounded arm gushed blood. John lost consciousness.

A couple of days passed, and the number of crosses had grown in the dog cemetery. The sun was setting, and the horizon was dark orange. The shadows of the crosses stretched across the rice paddy. Douglas stood in the background, saying his parting words as Titan was laid to rest.

"You're a lucky one. You get to go back home. I gotta stay here and fight in this shit," Gregory said to John.

"Nothing lucky about what happened to me. Fortunate, maybe, but not lucky. Besides, this shits over here. Everybody will be going home soon."

"Not soon enough. Not soon enough," Gregory responded.

They both saluted as a marine played his bugle.

"He's not as good as Smiles," John remarked.

"No way in hell," agreed Gregory.

They shared a quiet moment, remembering their fallen friends, their fallen marines.

16

A few weeks passed, and John made his way back to Camp Lejeune.

He walked up the steps and knocked on Emily's door, nervous to see his love but excited at the same time. She opened the door and was in complete and utter shock seeing him standing there. They embraced each other as he swung her around.

"I wasn't expecting you for a few more days! Oh, and look at me! Fresh out of bed. Your letter said next week. What a surprise!" Emily said as she hugged and kissed him repeatedly.

"Fresh out of bed? I can change that." His trademark crooked grin was hard for her to resist.

He picked her up, carried her inside, and shut the door behind him. They spent the remainder of the day indoors, in bed, making up for lost time, their

long-distance love finally reuniting in the small confines of a bedroom.

After reconditioning themselves to each other,
they turned their focus to Duke. His injuries from the
blast had healed up nicely; it was his emotional wounds
that needed attention. At the time, there were no real
reconditioning procedures or facilities for the dogs
that made it back to the States. John and Emily did it
themselves. They made sure to acclimate Duke to various people and situations. He was a bit shell-shocked
at first, running from the sound of a slamming door
or the backfiring of a car. His dreams caused him to
whine violently and thrash around, and they were certainly a sign that the war and his experiences had a
profound effect on him.

Many of the things Duke was experiencing were
also those that affected John. This put a lot of pressure
on Emily to help both of them. Her kind and caring
spirit helped all three cope with their new life and the
struggles that came with it. It was a tough process, a
long process with many ups and downs. Duke seemed
to adjust faster, and within a month he was ready to
return to his family, just as promised.

John contacted his father and asked if he could
come to North Carolina and stay for a few days. He
hadn't seen him since the day he left Little Rock, and
while they did keep in touch sporadically through
John's time in training and in the Pacific, they needed
to see each other. John needed to see his father and

tell him of his plans to make Emily an honest woman. He wanted his father to be there for that moment.

The axles on the old jeep creaked and squeaked as Emily, Roy, and John pulled up to the Johnson's house. They exited the vehicle and walked up to the door. With a deep breath, John knocked. Ty walked up from the basement. He wiped the grease from his hand, placed a wrench in his pocket, and opened the door.

Sherry walked up to his side. They noticed the covered marine jeep in the street as young Tommy walked up the pathway. A few prying neighbors stood on their porches watching. It wasn't every day that the marines were on their street.

"Good afternoon, sir, ma'am. We're from the US Marine Corps and Dogs for Defense," John explained.

Ty saluted and extended his hand. Roy and John saluted as well. This was the first time the two had had the opportunity to share this military tradition. They smiled at each other as they lowered their hands.

"I'm Ty Johnson, and this is my wife, Sherry. This here is our son, Tommy.

"Is Duke coming back?" Tommy asked.

"Tommy! Let the man speak," Sherry said quickly.

Tommy pulled a crumpled picture from his pocket, looked at it, and recognized that he was looking at

John Markle. "Private Markle!" Then Tommy, following his father's earlier lead, saluted.

"Good morning. This is Emily, and that is my father, Roy. Tommy, Duke served his country with honor. His accomplishments will never be forgotten. He saved many lives out there on the battlefield, and I can personally say that he earned this more than I did," explained John.

He pulled out his Silver Star and handed it to the young boy. "Son, this medal represents bravery and valor in battle. It was given to me, but Duke represents all the qualities of a hero, more so than me. He is a hero. He was one of the best dogs the marines will ever have the pleasure of working with. I want you to have this medal on behalf of Duke."

Tommy rubbed the Silver Star and stared at it, not breaking away from it until he heard John's voice again.

"Tommy, it is my pleasure to return Duke to you and your family."

John whistled loudly, and Duke jumped from the covered jeep and raced toward them. He ran straight for Tommy, and the little boy embraced his best friend. Then they immediately started to jump around together since it was, after all, a very happy reunion. Sherry and Emily hugged each other and cried as Ty, Roy, and John walked over to embrace everyone, including Duke and Tommy. They all took a seat in the front yard with Duke. It was nice under the shade of a large oak tree.

"Nice place you got here. Plenty of land," John said as he scanned the property.

"Just moved in a few months ago. We couldn't be happier. Job market finally came through," Ty explained.

Duke pulled Tommy around by a rope, just like old times. Tommy laughed hysterically as he passed by, happy to have his friend back. Just then Duke suddenly stopped and alerted. From behind the house appeared a beautiful female Doberman, red and rust in color.

"Oh, this is Cleo. Short for Cleopatra," Sherry explained.

Emily and John turned and looked at each other. They smiled warmly at each other.

John made eye contact with his father, who nodded at him, giving him the go-ahead with his plan. Roy jokingly whispered to him, "Go ahead, son. You made it through the war; you can certainly make it through marriage."

With that, John reached for Emily's hand. He stared at her, into her eyes, deep into her soul. He dropped to one knee, which instantly caused Sherry to gasp at what she was about to witness. She was so excited to be a part of this that her hands were shaking as she covered her mouth.

Everyone stopped and turned their attention to John and Emily. With a quiver in his throat, John began to speak from his heart. He held a little black box in one hand.

"Emily, I never thought I would meet someone like you. When I first saw you working with Duke, something grabbed my heart and pulled me across the field to you. It was in that moment that I knew you were special—someone very, very special—and you've inspired me to be a better person. Your generosity, just to volunteer your time to train those dogs, allowed me to see a glimpse of your soul and your heart that day. I missed you every day I was out there. Your letters and your life carried me through many of the hard times. The story of our love is just the beginning. Let's write the happy ending together. I cannot imagine growing old with anyone else but you. I love you with all my heart, and I will for all eternity. Emily, will you make me the happiest man on earth? Will you marry me?"

He opened the little box, revealing a ring—a ring very familiar to his family. It belonged to his mother, and with his father's blessing, he now offered this ring to the woman he had fallen in love with. It was beautiful. A rose-cut diamond was housed in the middle of the Edwardian-style ring. It was adorned with magnificent, brilliant sapphires that were embedded in the filigree detailing crafted into the platinum mountings.

With her eyes welling up with tears of joy, Emily accepted his offer. Roy wiped a tear from his eye. He stood proud as John slid the ring onto Emily's finger.

The entire group clapped and yelled just as the ring reached its resting place on her hand. John vowed never to leave her again. Duke and Cleo sat next to each other, and of course, Tommy was right next to them. Ty and Sherry stood hand-in-hand, watching the young couple start their lives with each other.

Roy loved seeing his son happy and in love. He had always told John that, just as it says in the Bible, love conquers all and is the most important thing to a happy life. He looked at everyone and then glanced up at the large, protecting branches of the old oak tree. The shade from the tree and the cool breeze flowing through the leaves let Roy know that he wasn't alone.

The End

Printed in Germany
by Amazon Distribution
GmbH, Leipzig